Realistic Scenery for Toy Train Layouts

DAVE FRARY

Photography by Dave Frary, unless otherwise noted

GREENBERG BOOKS

A Division of Kalmbach Publishing Co.

Printed in the United States of America

Publisher's Cataloging in Publication
(Prepared by Quality Books Inc.)

Frary, James David.
 Realistic scenery for toy train layouts / James David Frary.
  p. cm.
  Includes index.

  1. Railroads—Models. I. Title

TF197.F68 1996   625.1'9
                        QBI96-40050

Art Director: Kristi Ludwig
Book Design: Mark Watson

Contents

Foreword

Toy train operators have come to appreciate the dramatic impact that realistic scenery can add to layouts of any size, scale, or gauge. Considering the deluge of well-detailed semi-scale locomotives and cars manufactured today, it's understandable why you want more than a coat of green paint as your layout scenery! What you really want is believable scenery that's just as intriguing as the toy trains that run around the layout.

Some layout operators mistakenly think that they must purchase every commercial scenery product available to create realistic scenery. Those who do concoct scenery this way are usually discouraged by the amount of money they spend to achieve only mediocre results. But for most operators who create it methodically, using common products and materials, scenery is typically the least expensive and most rewarding component of any layout.

Layout scenery doesn't have to be elaborate or expensive, but it must be effective and easy to build. Simple, effective scenery can provide some ingenious ways to disguise exposed benchwork or wires, switch machines, track actuators, signals, and other unrealistic elements inherent to toy trains. And as a functional part of your layout, scenery also helps to protect your treasured toy trains by keeping them from falling to the floor if they derail.

In the pages that follow, you'll discover numerous proven, easy-to-follow scenery techniques developed by one of the best craftsmen in the hobby of model railroading. As you work your way through these steps you'll also learn that you really don't have to be an artist to produce satisfying results. Then you'll know you're well on your way to building some truly impressive and original scenery for your toy train layout!

—*Kent Johnson*

Using the tools, materials, tips, and techniques that follow, you'll create realistic and interesting scenery that you and your guest will enjoy.

1 Tools and Materials

For many toy train operators, building scenery is the part of layout construction they fear the most. Just keep one thing in mind—building scenery doesn't have to be an artistic endeavor. From the planning stages until you fix the final detail on your layout,

Tools

This is a list of tools I used to build the scenery in this book. Most of the items are common household or construction tools, so check around your home before you go shopping. At the end of this book you'll also find a list of manufacturers and suppliers for some of the items listed below.

Carpenter's Tools
- ✓ ½" wood chisel
- ✓ Carpenter's square
- ✓ Caulking gun
- ✓ Cutting pliers
- ✓ Hacksaw blade
- ✓ Level
- ✓ Long-nosed pliers
- ✓ Makita 5090D circular hand saw
- ✓ Sanding block (medium sandpaper)
- ✓ Stanley Surform tool
- ✓ Staple gun
- ✓ Straightedge
- ✓ Wood rasp

Household Items
- ✓ 16-ounce plant sprayer
- ✓ Aluminum foil
- ✓ Black permanent marker
- ✓ Disposable cups
- ✓ Disposable latex gloves
- ✓ Eyedropper
- ✓ Hairbrush
- ✓ Lead weights
- ✓ No. 80437 Bright Bar track-cleaning block from Micro-Mark
- ✓ Phillips-head screwdriver
- ✓ Scissors
- ✓ Shaving brush
- ✓ Strainer
- ✓ Tea strainer
- ✓ Turkey baster
- ✓ Wooden tongue depressor

Cutting Tools
- ✓ Hobby knife
- ✓ Linoleum knife
- ✓ Palette knife
- ✓ Serrated-edge knife

Painting Tools
- ✓ 1½"-, 3"-, and 4"-wide brushes
- ✓ Disposable foam brush
- ✓ No. 11 round-tip sable brush
- ✓ No. 12 square-tip nylon brush, ½" wide
- ✓ Paint rollers and trays
- ✓ Respirator

you'll find that scenery building is fun and easy if you follow the methods presented here.

The techniques in this book have been applied by thousands of model railroaders who have achieved pleasing, consistent results. The formula for success is simple. Read through the step-by-step procedures, gather the tools and materials, and then start your scenery.

Scenery building is very forgiving and you won't be disappointed. You'll create realistic and interesting scenery for your trains to run through and viewers to appreciate.

For years I've kept a notebook of ideas about building scenery. If an idea is easy and it works well, I write it down. In the back of the notebook I have a list of tips and techniques that others have shared with me. They are particularly valuable because they usually provide a different slant on a method of construction or a problem in scenery building. If you haven't started your own notebook yet, then try some ideas from mine. They will get you headed in the right direction.

As you use these techniques, try altering them to suit your special requirements. Remember, this is now your guide to creating scenery for your own toy train layout—so when you

Materials

Here's the list of materials I used to build the scenery in this book. Again, most of the items are common household or construction materials. The manufacturers and suppliers listed at the end of the book will help you find some of the items.

Adhesives, Compounds, and Binders
- ✓ ½" staples
- ✓ 3M Super 77 spray adhesive
- ✓ Aleene's Original tacky glue
- ✓ Elmer's Weather-Tite wood glue
- ✓ Hob-e-Tac adhesive
- ✓ Liquid Nails adhesive
- ✓ Phillips pan-head ¾" no. 4 track screws
- ✓ Pre-mixed joint compound or spackle
- ✓ Scotch Guard
- ✓ Seam tape
- ✓ Super-hold hair spray
- ✓ Two-part, 5-minute epoxy
- ✓ White glue

Paint and Coloring
- ✓ Acrylic colors: medium blue, green, black, and white
- ✓ Design Master spray paints
- ✓ Earth-color latex wall paint
- ✓ Flat black paint
- ✓ Flat blue paint
- ✓ Flat white in a spray can
- ✓ Flat white paint
- ✓ Floquil rail brown
- ✓ Gloss medium
- ✓ Gray primer in a spray can
- ✓ Grumbacher soft pastels, catalog no. 00/L
- ✓ Polly S boxcar red, reefer white, blue, and green
- ✓ Sears no. 125 royal blue medium bright
- ✓ Tinting colors

Scenery Elements
- ✓ 1" square pine strips
- ✓ ¼" foam-core board (sometimes sold under the name Fome-Cor)
- ✓ Baseball diamond clay or other fine material for texture
- ✓ Cheesecloth
- ✓ Dishwashing detergent
- ✓ Evergreen .010" styrene
- ✓ Komatex plastic sheet (4 by 8-foot sheet, 3 millimeters thick)
- ✓ Latex molding rubber by AMACO (American Art Clay Company)
- ✓ Lionel 6-12734 passenger/freight station
- ✓ Lionel 6-62716 short extension bridge
- ✓ Mountains in Minutes mold release concentrate
- ✓ Mountains in Minutes Polyfoam, parts A and B
- ✓ Natural Aggregates ballast
- ✓ Plaster of paris
- ✓ Real dirt
- ✓ Scenic foam grass
- ✓ Sculptamold
- ✓ Styrofoam insulation board
- ✓ Timber Products Bridgemaster heavy duty truss components
- ✓ Twig trees
- ✓ Variety of scenic foam colors, coarse and fine texture
- ✓ Woodland Scenics FC58 medium green foliage clusters
- ✓ Woodland Scenics FP178 Poly Fiber

come across something that works, jot it down in the margins.

All the supplies you need to build scenery are available at hardware and home improvement shops or craft and hobby shops. I've purposely selected materials that are easy to find and will give you great results. There's always a sense of accomplishment when you can start and finish a project that adds to the realistic appearance of your layout.

Adding ties and ballasting the track can provide extra realism. You can buy commercial products or use ¼" foam-core board for the ties and aquarium gravel for the ballast.

2 Tracklaying and Ballasting

Laying the track is the part of building any layout that usually goes the fastest—yet many train enthusiasts never get beyond this step. I'll show you a fast and painless way to mount the track permanently, then add ties and ballast for extra realism.

TRACKLAYING AND ROADBED TIPS

The first step is to lay out the track sections and test-fit them in position.

This is the time to make any adjustments and make decisions—will you use odd lengths, cut to fit, or stay with the standard factory pieces? It's important to ensure that parallel tracks really are square and true, and that the curved track sections are firmly pushed together. I use a 3-foot-long yardstick and a carpenter's square to help keep everything in alignment.

When all the track pieces are where you want them, temporarily screw the

Half-inch-long staples will hold the roadbed flat while the glue dries. The staples will not be seated flush, making it easier to remove them later.

track in place, fastening only every fifth or sixth section. This will keep the track flat and firm for the next step, which is outlining each track component with a black marking pen. After you've drawn the complete outline, remove the track in clusters of three or four sections. Store them flat on the floor or under the layout, ready to reinstall after the roadbed is in place.

I mount the track on cork roadbed, which provides a firm, smooth base and absorbs some—but not all—of the noise generated by the train. Strip the cork apart down the middle and reverse one section. When you reassemble it with the square edges abutting in the middle, the roadbed is 2½" wide, just about the same width as the metal ties that are crimped to the rails. This means the track outline you drew can serve as a guide for positioning the cork.

Apply a wide ribbon of white glue within the track outline, then work each half of the cork roadbed into place, aligning each outer edge with the outline. Use ½" staples to hold

the roadbed flat and in place while the glue dries. Tip up the front of the staple gun about ⅛" from the surface of the cork, then drive the staple. Since you're holding the gun slightly off the cork the staples are not seated flush, making them easy to remove later. After the glue dries I use long-nosed pliers to pull the staples while holding the cork firm on either side of the staple.

When you've removed all the staples, it's time to level the surface of the cork roadbed. Make a sanding block from a scrap of 2 x 4 wrapped in a sheet of coarse sandpaper, then sand in the long direction. The roadbed doesn't need a lot of sanding—just enough to remove any bumps and smooth the surface to make it level.

OVER THE RIVER . . .

At one spot on my layout I planned to have a river passing under the track. Because the river would run on the layout surface I had to raise the track. I cut along either side of the cork roadbed with a small circular saw. After cutting, I raised the cork

Using a small battery-operated circular saw, cut along either side of the cork roadbed to raise it for the bridge.

Use wooden blocks to raise the roadbed 2½". Next, smear them with glue and position them under the roadbed, then apply weights until the glue dries.

Add foam-core ties between the metal ties on each section of Lionel track. Use Elmer's Weather-Tite wood glue to hold the ties in place because it's water resistant. Make a tie-spacing gauge out of a length of plastic to show where to place the ties.

roadbed and the plywood under it, using blocks of wood to hold it at the right height.

I needed a 2½" rise, so I cut several wooden blocks to that height. I smeared them with glue and positioned them under the roadbed. I placed weights on top of the roadbed until the glue dried. Later I reinforced the glue with long drywall screws through the roadbed into the blocks.

BACK ON TRACK

Now you can replace the track sections for good, using pan-head no. 4 x ¾" Phillips screws to anchor them firmly to the roadbed. The outline you used to position the roadbed also serves as a guide for laying the track.

Use a small brush to paint both sides of the rail with Floquil rail brown. It's important to apply the paint on the rail flange, the part of the rail most folks see first. After the paint dries, clean the rail tops. I used a no. 80437 Bright Bar track-cleaning block from Micro-Mark. The block is large enough to clean three rails at once.

I wanted more ties under the rail than the three or four metal ones that are furnished on each section. A number of manufacturers offer additional ties made of wood or plastic (see Appendix). Because these extra ties are just for looks, you can also make them out of almost anything. I had a sheet of black ¼"-thick foam-core board on hand, so that's what I used. Foam core is a thin sheet of foam sandwiched between two sheets of posterboard. It's sold in stationery, graphic art, and art supply stores. With a hobby knife and straightedge, cut strips ½" wide, then chop the strips into 2" lengths.

I added three additional foam-core ties between the metal ties on each straight section and two on the curved pieces. Pour a little Elmer's Weather-Tite Wood Glue (water-resistant when it dries, so it won't soften when the ballast is glued in place) into the plastic lid of a coffee can.

Dip the far end of each tie into a little of the glue and slide it into place under the rail. The sliding motion

Paint all the chrome Phillips-head screws flat black so they'll blend with the track.

spreads the glue evenly along the length of the tie.

To space the ties evenly, make a rulerlike jig out of a length of plastic with evenly spaced marks to show where the ties are to go. Set the jig against the edge of the rail and place the ties so they align with the marks.

After all the ties are in place, go around the layout and paint all the bright chrome track screws flat black.

SPREADING BALLAST

Before applying the ballast, check all the electrical connections for good contact. Once the ballast is in place it's hard to correct bad connections.

Selecting the right ballast can be fun! While hobby shops carry a tremendous variety of realistic crushed stone ballast, I decided to try something different. Being a tropical fish nut, I frequent the pet supply store as

Use Natural Aggregates aquarium stones for the ballast and spread them with a paper coffee cup. The cup can be squeezed to shape to get the ballast to flow where it's needed.

Spread the ballast stones using a large soft brush. It's important to check the inside rails for ballast stones that may interfere with train operation.

often as the hobby shop. I found a variety of stones sold as "Natural Aggregates" for decorating aquariums, fish bowls and dish gardens. They come in a large selection of sizes and colors perfect for tinplate and large scale layouts. I bought several bags of reddish brown stones about 1/8" in diameter. They're also coated, which makes them clean enough to be applied to the track without washing them first.

Use a paper coffee cup to spread the ballast. The paper is soft enough that you can squeeze and shape the cup rim to conform to the width between the rails and to get into all those tight places, such as around the switches.

Spread the stones between the rails and along the outside edges. Use a large soft brush to distribute the ballast evenly, removing any that might interfere with train operation. Take your time spreading the ballast, because once it's glued in place it'll be there for good.

CEMENTING THE DEAL

Mix three parts water and one part white glue in a large screw-topped jar.

This will be your track cement. Pre-wet the ballast with a light misting of water from a plant sprayer (add a few drops of liquid dishwashing detergent to make the water flow).

Using a turkey baster or large eye-dropper, drizzle the glue down the middle of the track, between the ties. The solution should flow evenly to both sides of the track. If it doesn't, apply more water spray and glue until

After the ballast is where you want it, spray it with "wet water" made by adding a few drops of liquid dishwashing detergent to 16 ounces of water. The wet water helps the ballast glue flow around each stone.

Use a large eye-dropper to spread the dilute white glue over the ballast. Soak the ballast until the glue runs out of the stones, then allow the ballast to dry undisturbed overnight.

the ballast is saturated with the glue mix. Wipe up any that runs off with paper towels, then allow the ballast to dry undisturbed overnight.

Before running a train you'll have to clean the rail tops thoroughly with a track-cleaning block. Run your forefinger along the inside edge of both outer rails to check for ballast grains that could cause derailments.

For extra realism, weather the ballast with a black wash: 1 tablespoon india ink to 1 quart water, plus

The finished ballast is strong and durable, and it really holds the tracks in place.

After the glue dries, weather the edges of the ballast with a wash made of earth-color latex paint and water. The wash simulates the dulling effects of rain and snow.

Toolbox of equipment

To lay the cork roadbed:
- ✓ Straightedge
- ✓ Carpenter's square
- ✓ Black permanent marker
- ✓ Hobby knife
- ✓ White glue
- ✓ Staple gun
- ✓ ½" staples
- ✓ Long-nosed pliers
- ✓ Sanding block (medium sandpaper)
- ✓ Linoleum knife or circular handsaw
- ✓ Lead weights

To lay the track and ballast:
- ✓ Small paintbrush
- ✓ Bright Bar track-cleaning block
- ✓ Phillips-head screwdriver
- ✓ Phillips pan-head ¾" no. 4 track screws
- ✓ Hobby knife
- ✓ Wood glue
- ✓ Disposable cups
- ✓ Large, soft paintbrush
- ✓ White glue (diluted)
- ✓ Turkey baster

several drops of liquid detergent so it will flow better. Soak a large brush in the wash and flow it down the center of the track. In a yard or heavy traffic area you may want to make several applications until the ballast looks really dirty.

I weather the outer edges of the ballast with an earth-color wash. Add ⅛ cup earth-color paint to 1 quart water. Flow this along either side of the rail to subdue the ballast color and show the effects of rain and snow.

Thick, lush-looking ground cover will take your scenery out of the humdrum and propel it into the extraordinary.

3 Applying Ground Cover

Now that the track is in place and the trains are running, it's time to start the scenery. Set your accessories in place, draw lines around their bases, and remove them to a safe place until after the scenery is complete. This is also a good time to run wires to power these accessories.

You can tack the wires to the surface of the layout with hot glue or lead them through predrilled holes. I like to put a knob of masking tape on the stripped ends of the wires so they don't get lost during scenery construction. Also check the wires to the track. Cover them with tape to keep them

To make realistic ground cover on your layout, you'll need an assortment of green and yellow-green scenic foam. Select both fine and coarse textures.

from working loose. Now you can start the scenery, knowing you've minimized the potential for electrical problems later on.

There are two common ways to add ground texture to a tinplate layout. The simplest is to paint the areas between the tracks with green paint and sprinkle green sawdust over it while it's wet. This is fine for a holiday layout that gets put away a few weeks after New Year's, but if you'd like realistic ground cover, there is so much more you can do with just a little more work. The second method requires more effort, but is well worth it if you're building a permanent layout.

Start by gathering materials. A trip to the hobby shop will allow you to choose among many colors and textures of scenic ground cover. You'll want to choose scenic foam in several basic green colors to start with. Buy both fine and coarse textures, if they're available. The basic greens you choose now will be become the base color for the whole layout, so try to choose a name brand that will be around for several years.

Also buy an assortment of the lighter shades of green and yellow-

green scenic foam. They will help to brighten the layout under relatively weak indoor lighting and will improve realism as well. Purchase an assortment of weed material, several tree kits, and a couple of packages of brown or dead-leaf-colored foam. As for the other materials you'll eventually need, you can buy them now or gather them later, as they're needed. See the list of tools and materials in this chapter.

You'll also need an assortment of fine dirt that matches the earth colors of your favorite railroad.

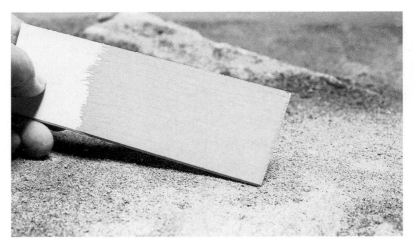

A good way to find an appropriate earth color for your layout is to make a color chip of your favorite earth-color hobby paint. Take this chip to the paint store for a color match.

CHOOSING AN EARTH COLOR

Before applying the grass and dirt, paint the scenery base an earth color. Choosing the color is important, since you'll use it as the base color for all earth and rocks on the layout.

Earth-color paints from the hobby shop are fine for small displays, but get very expensive when you're building a layout. Instead, head for the paint store. Select a shade of flat interior latex wall paint that's close to the dirt color in the area you're modeling.

A layout set in New England, for instance, should feature a basic gray-brown color typical of the flinty soil found there. For the Southwest, light reds, yellows, and beige colors should predominate. If your layout is freelance, make a color chip from your favorite earth-color hobby paint. Take that to the paint store for a match.

If you're lucky enough to live near the railroad you're modeling, you can match the earth color exactly. Glue some fine, oven-dried dirt on a white card to make a color sample. Take it to the paint store and have them match it with their cheapest flat indoor latex.

If you're not close to the area you're modeling, you'll have to determine the colors of dirt, ballast, and gravel by observing color photos or guessing. Some modelers buy fine gravel or ballast at the hobby shop and use this as the basis for choosing a base color.

GATHERING DIRT FOR TEXTURE

Making your own dirt texture is cheap (cheap as dirt!) and enables you to find a latex paint to match. Being a frugal Yankee, I always travel with a small scoop and several empty coffee cans with snap-on lids. Wherever I see a new color or texture along the roadside I stop and fill the cans. When I get home I spread the dirt on several layers of newspaper in the cellar to dry. Some folks bake the dirt in a low oven to dry it and to kill the bugs. When the dirt is dry sift it into fine and coarse grades through two screens that have meshes of different size.

An inexpensive alternative to scooping dirt from the side of the road is to buy a bag of contractor's sand from a builder's supply store. Contractor's sand usually matches several popular earth-color hobby paints, and can be sifted into several grades.

ADDING THE TEXTURE

Now that you have selected a paint and texture material that match, you can begin coloring the scenery base. If

Scenery glue

Use scenery glue, or bonding agent, to hold more texture in place. Make it by mixing one part white glue with three parts water. (Don't use a carpenter's glue or other thick yellow glue. It doesn't mix well with water.) Add several drops of liquid dishwashing detergent to the mixture, pour it into a large plastic container with a screw-top lid, and give it a good shaking to mix it.

The solids in the glue will settle, so you'll have to shake or stir the container before each use. The best way to apply the glue is with a wide brush, a turkey baster, or an eyedropper, depending on how much material you're gluing in place. I've also used a squeeze-bottle mustard dispenser purchased at a dollar store—it's ideal when I need to apply a small dab of glue. You'll also need some "wet water." Fill a 16-ounce pump-type plant sprayer with water and add several drops of liquid detergent. I will recommend using wet water throughout this book to pre-wet texture material before applying glue.

Use earth-color paint as a scenery sealer and as the glue to hold the first layer of texture. Apply plenty of full-strength paint and work in small sections before the paint dries.

Make a texture sprinkler by punching holes in the plastic top of a coffee can.

the scenery on your layout will be flat, without hills or mountains, then begin by coloring the tabletop. Apply plenty of full-strength earth-color paint to cover and seal the layout base. Don't brush it out! It should be thick, but not puddling. I like to use a cheap disposable foam brush for this step because it allows me to flow on lots of paint.

Next, sprinkle a base coat of texture over the wet paint. It can be green grass alone, grass and fine gravel, or mostly gravel, depending on where your railroad operates. Gather your scenic foam grass and different gravel textures. I store each in its own coffee can with a snap-on lid.

To sprinkle the texture you can use coffee cans with holes poked in the lid, empty spice jars, or any type of kitchen sifter. Sifting with your fingers works great, too, but is time-consuming—and it takes some practice to spread the texture evenly.

Work in one small area at a time to ensure that the paint is still wet as you apply the texture over it. Spread the paint and sprinkle the grass evenly, trying to cover the earth-color paint completely. The texture will adhere to the paint somewhat unevenly,

After the paint dries, pass the nozzle of a vacuum cleaner close to the foam to remove any loose texture.

19

To fill large areas with dense undergrowth, use Woodland Scenics Foliage Net. Stretch the netting as thin as possible, apply white glue full strength, and push the netting into it.

To add touches of color to the foliage, spray the surface lightly with superhold hair spray and sprinkle on brightly colored red and yellow foam to make flowers.

giving the landscape a more realistic look. Add a sprinkle of gravel here and there to create variety. Continue applying paint and sprinkling texture until the tabletop is covered. Let the paint dry overnight.

Now pass the nozzle of a vacuum cleaner close to—but not touching—the layout surface to remove loose texture. If you'd like to save some of the texture, sweep it from the layout surface with a large, clean paintbrush. Push all the texture off the edge of the layout into a can. Then vacuum the layout. Don't be concerned if there are a few bare spots—you'll fix this by adding more texture.

Sprinkle on more texture material as needed. Think of the texture as being applied in layers; the more layers you apply, the more detailed (and realistic) the scene will look. I like the texture to be thick in fields and

meadows, and fine around the tracks.

Work in small, manageable areas. Use a large, soft brush to push the texture and ground cover around until it rests exactly where you want it. then hold it in place with wet-water spray. The trick is to mist on water just until the texture snuggles down. The wet water provides a path that carries the glue into and throughout the texture.

Next, drizzle on the dilute scenery glue. Add sufficient glue to soak all the texture thoroughly. Don't be concerned if you apply a little too much and it runs into unwanted areas. To absorb it you can use a swatch of paper towel or simply apply more texture.

You'll usually need additional dirt and grass around structures and accessories after setting them in place. Small patches of grass or weeds, a pile of gravel, and leaves around the foundation are all prototypical. I sprinkle the texture around the structures with my fingers, then push it into place with a soft brush. Keep brushing and pushing until it looks perfect. This is one place where I take my time to get all the texture just right.

With the texture in place around the base, use an eyedropper to drip on wet water. Apply glue until the texture has absorbed it all. Again, you can cover small puddles of excess glue

Lichen is an old-time tree-making material that's been a standby for many years. Spruce up plain lichen by dipping each piece in dilute white glue, squeezing out excess, and rolling in scenic foam. After the pieces dry, trim the ragged edges, cut a flat spot on the bottom, and glue in place.

A great way to model a wheat field or tall grass is to use fake fur. Here a piece has been glued to the scenic base. The next step will be to add scenic foam around the field, then texture and color it.

The best place for a field is next to the farm. Here the field is surrounded by bushes and trees. Mat the fur to look like dead grass that has been knocked over by the wind.

Make the high grass in this cemetery from a small swatch of fake fur. Color it with a green felt-tip pen and sprinkle it with chopped lichen.

Flocking makes great foreground grass. It's easy to apply. Just shake the flocking over the ground that's been wet with dilute white glue.

can without tearing it. Work over a sheet of newspaper. (The newspaper will catch all the foam that falls off, which you can save and reuse.) Stretch the pieces, then pull off a hunk and roll it into a loose ball. Dip the bottom of the ball into a dish of dilute glue and set it in place on the scenery.

Apply the foliage net ball so that the top is elevated and it has a "see-through" look. The bottom should rest flat on the scenic base so that the glue will stick. To cover large areas, stretch the foliage net as thin as possible and push it into the ground, which you have painted with dilute white glue. For touches of extra color, plant flowers by sprinkling bright red or yellow foam over the netting.

with more texture or sponge them away with the corner of a paper towel.

Arrange details such as tree limbs and branches, bushes, small stones, and other junk on top of the grass and dirt, then glue them as described above. Heavy details need a drop of full-strength white glue on the bottom to hold them.

MODELING DENSE UNDERGROWTH

To create the illusion of dense undergrowth and to add height to a flat meadow I use Woodland Scenics Foliage Net—a soft, hairlike netting that has scenic foam glued to it. It's sold in several summer and fall colors.

Stretch the netting as thin as you

USING LICHEN

Model denser undergrowth using shredded lichen. Lichen (pronounced lie-ken) is a preserved natural growth available in most hobby shops. As it comes from the package, you can use lichen for tall bushes and shrubs, but it also makes great-looking undergrowth. Rip the lichen into small pieces and glue them to the scenery base or, for extra texture, dip each piece in dilute white glue, squeeze out excess glue, and roll in scenic foam. Set them aside to dry overnight. To use, just trim the ragged edges, cut a flat spot on the bottom, and glue in place.

A dry wash can add interest to a plain area on your layout. Start by digging a trench in the scenery down to the Styrofoam base. It's easy to do with a sharp serrated-edge knife.

MODELING FIELD CROPS WITH FUR

Fake fur can easily be used to model a field of wheat or other tall grass. This is sold in fabric stores by the yard, and a yard is enough for half a dozen layouts. Select a brownish gold or light beige dead-grass color.

Start by cutting a piece of fake fur slightly larger than the field you want. Lay it flat on the workbench and comb out the loose hairs with an old hairbrush. This step may take several tries, but you'll want to remove as much loose fiber as possible. Be careful, though—you can remove too much fur and make bald spots in your fields.

To eliminate wrinkles or folds, wet the fur swatch under running water and lay it flat on an old towel. Place small weights on each corner to hold it flat until it's dry.

While it dries, you can tint the tips of the fur to look like new grass or ripening grain. Put a few drops of Polly S field green or other acrylic yellow-green color on a damp paper towel or soft brush and wipe it gently over the tops of the fur fibers. If you apply too much color just take a dry pad of paper towel and wipe the excess away. After the grass dries more color can be applied if necessary.

The best way to install your wheat field is to apply a thick coat of white glue on the base and press the fur into it. Add small weights (the same ones you used while the fur was drying) along the edges to hold the fur flat. After the glue dries remove the weights.

Detail the field by sprinkling fine sand over the fur and brushing the sand into the nap so that most of it ends up on the ground. Mist with wet water and drizzle on dilute glue. You can place hedgerows, stone walls, or fences around the edges to protect your crop from roving animals.

MODELING TALL GRASS WITH FLOCKING

An easy-to-use substitute for fake fur is flocking, a finely chopped arti-

ficial fiber colored to look like green, yellow, or brown grass.

The grass it makes isn't as tall as that made with fur, but flocking is about the right height to make a rough lawn in O scale. Apply it with any kind of shaker over an area that you have sprayed with wet water and drizzled with dilute glue. Use it in the foreground of the layout, where it will be seen.

MODELING A DRY WASH

Another easy ground cover disguised as a detailed scenery area is a dry wash. This is a dry stream bed, which you can locate anywhere water would naturally flow.

Start by digging a trench in the scenery base. If you're using Styrofoam, cut

To hold the stones that will rest in the wash, brush on full-strength white glue. When working with this glue, keep a jar of clean water handy for cleaning the brush.

Toolbox of equipment

To apply ground cover:
✓ Disposable foam brush
✓ Tea strainer
✓ White glue
✓ Large, soft paintbrush
✓ Eyedropper
✓ 16-ounce plant sprayer
✓ Hairbrush
✓ Lead weights
✓ Serrated-edge knife

Sprinkle the largest stones into the wet glue. Gather these by sifting a bag of contractor's sand through a window screen.

After large stones are in place, wet them and add the smaller ones. The wet water lets the glue flow around the rocks.

a long thin wedge in the shape of the stream bed. Coat it with earth-color paint and allow to dry.

Brush full-strength white glue into the stream and sprinkle on the largest stones first. Follow these with smaller stones, then sprinkle fine sand over the whole wash. Brush the sand from the tops of the stones into the spaces between them. Use the brush to move the stones and sand into their final resting places. Mist the stones with wet water and squirt on dilute white glue.

After the glue dries add details like weeds, stumps, branches, dead wood, and old tires to make your dry stream bed come alive.

To fill the spaces between the large rocks, use the same stones as you used for ballast. To finish the wash, sprinkle on fine sand and brush it into the spaces between the stones. The rocks are held in place with dilute glue.

Complex-looking rock work, here almost hidden by the dense undergrowth, gives a subtle realism to any hi-rail layout.

4 Making Mountains and Rocks

The first scenic feature added to most toy train layouts is a tunnel, often a ready-made one that looks like a loaf of bread. Traditionally, a hobbyist drops it over one corner of the track to provide visual interest on an otherwise flat landscape.

But you can go beyond the portable tunnel and create permanent, realistic hills and mountains. I'll briefly

An inexpensive and lightweight way to form scenic contours is by using cardboard strips. Cut these 1" strips from the side of a box using a hobby knife and straightedge.

describe a couple of traditional techniques you may want to try, but then I'll provide full instructions for building hills with foam insulation board.

PLASTER OVER WIRE SCREENING

Veterans of the model train hobby may remember building a scenic base from scraps of wood, with window screening formed into domes and valleys and tacked to it. Builders troweled plaster of paris over the screening, then colored and detailed the hardened shell.

This was a good way to produce permanent, substantial scenery that would last for generations—and some of it did. The plaster was easy to paint and rocks could be carved into its surface while it cured. The materials were—and are—cheap and easy to find. And beginning modelers could achieve good results.

On the down side, plaster over screen wire makes heavy scenery, and building it creates quite a mess. The screen wire reinforcement makes it hard to change contours without ripping the structures out and starting again. You have only ten minutes or so to work the plaster, which means you have to work pretty fast in small areas.

PLASTER-SOAKED PAPER TOWELS OVER CARDBOARD STRIPS

Over many years of experimenting, the plaster-over-wire-screen method evolved into a lightweight way to build scenery. One-inch wide cardboard strips replaced the screening. They make a fast, lightweight scenic base that you can shape and change at will. The strips can be fastened to any type of support with white glue, hot glue, or staples. Dip hand-sized pieces of

Weave together the shaped and twisted cardboard strips to make the desired contours. Held in place with glue or staples, they make a lightweight scenic base that you can reshape and change with very little work.

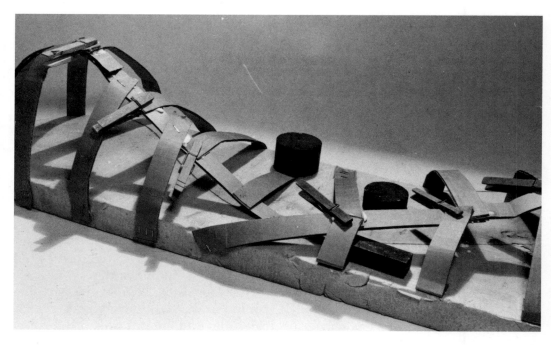

heavy paper towels in soupy plaster, then drape them across the cardboard frame, overlapping each by about a third. When the plaster sets, the structure is a strong, thin, lightweight shell.

This scenery is inexpensive to build and well suited to a permanent home layout, but it will not withstand the rigors of movement as on a modular or portable layout.

STYROFOAM INSULATION BOARD

Styrofoam board is one of the newest materials for scenery bases. Builders and contractors use it to insulate flat exterior and interior surfaces. They use construction adhesive or mastic to glue it in place. Most building supply stores and lumber yards sell it in 2 x 8-foot sheets 1" or 2" thick.

The easiest way to use Styrofoam insulation board to make hills and mountains is to stack the sheets on top of one another. The pile, which looks like a crude layer cake, need only be in the rough shape of hills and mountains; you'll smooth and shape the contours later.

The hills can be either solid or hollow. Solid hills are best if the hill is small or if you need extra strength.

Making foam mountains removable

Often you'll want to make parts of your mountains removable. It is worth the extra work, especially in areas you must be able to reach for routine maintenance or to rerail a runaway car or locomotive.

The easiest way to make a Styrofoam mountain removable is to omit the glue between two of the layers of foam. I insert finish nails to hold the foam in place while I finish the surrounding scenery. After the scenic contours are completed and the trees and grass are in place, I run a thin-bladed knife around the seam to loosen it, then lift the top from the mountain.

Hollow hills work best when you're building a large mountain. You can use all the Styrofoam pieces cut from the centers of the big mountain layers to make smaller hills, so there's a minimum of waste.

My favorite tools for cutting Styrofoam are a kitchen knife and a hacksaw blade. To cut long, straight pieces of foam board I like a serrated-edge paring knife with a 3" blade. I use it cocked at a 45-degree angle against a carpenter's square. Two or three swipes produce a straight, smooth cut.

This cross-section view shows what a great lightweight scenery support Styrofoam insulation board makes. It's available in building supply stores and lumber yards in 2 x 8-foot sheets, 1" or 2" thick.

The best way to cut Styrofoam is with a serrated kitchen knife with a 3" blade and a straightedge or carpenter's square.

Use a hacksaw blade with electrical tape wrapped around one end for cutting freehand shapes and irregular contours in Styrofoam. Use a serrated kitchen knife with a 3" blade for straight or square cuts.

For cutting freehand shapes and irregular contours and for removing excess material I like a hacksaw blade with electrical tape wrapped around one end to make a handle. Use short, quick strokes to make scroll and angle cuts; long strokes will tend to bind the blade and make it bend or break.

GLUING FOAM LAYERS

Once you've cut the rough shapes, hold the Styrofoam layers in place with white glue or foam-compatible construction adhesive. I prefer Liquid Nails because I can apply it with a caulking gun. Squeeze a bead on one surface and push the pieces together to spread the glue. The adhesive has enough body to hold the pieces together on its own, so you can keep working. You may have to hold a few heavy pieces in place overnight with long nails, weights, or clamps.

SHAPING STYROFOAM

After the glue dries you can begin to shape and smooth the Styrofoam to make the rough scenic contours.

There's no right or wrong way to do this—just remove enough material until the contours look good to you.

Three tools that I use for smoothing are a wire brush mounted in a power drill, a coarse-toothed wood rasp, and a Stanley Surform tool. The wire brush goes fastest; it shaves away lots of foam quickly, but it makes a big mess. Have a vacuum cleaner handy, preferably a heavy-duty shop vacuum, to suck up the bits of foam before they escape.

I like the wood rasp for fine shaping in areas near the edge of the layout or around tunnel portals—wherever you need control of the cutting. For smoothing large, broad areas the Stanley Surform tool is best. It's used like the wood rasp, but does not cut as fast.

CONTOUR WITH SCULPTAMOLD, THEN COLOR

After smoothing the foam I apply a thin layer of Sculptamold, a commercial scenery and sculpting mix, to seal the surface before painting. Sculptamold is a mixture of fiber, clay, and adhesive. It's one of the few scenery materials that will bond to the foam. (Plaster and papier maché can chip, crack, and work loose.) I mix Sculptamold with water to produce a soupy, plasterlike mixture that can be brushed or troweled over preshaped foam.

When the Sculptamold is dry I color it with an earth shade of flat interior latex paint, thinned with equal parts of water so that it will flow over the rough surface. I apply the earth color with a cheap, wide brush, "scrubbing" the paint on in some places to get it into all the cracks and crevices.

Since premixed wallboard joint compound will stick to the Styrofoam, you can substitute it for Sculptamold, but if you apply it too thickly, it will shrink and crack. Mixing dilute white glue with the joint compound can prevent shrinkage if you apply the compound in a layer less than ⅜" thick.

After gluing the layers of Styrofoam together, start the shaping process by removing the large areas with the hacksaw blade or knife.

ROCKIN' AND ROLLIN'

The rock formations on your layout will go a long way toward making your scenery believable, so it makes sense to spend a little extra time on them. Rock carving or molding followed by careful painting will separate your scenery from everyone else's.

Most folks shy away from carving rocks, because carving carries with it the connotation of artistic ability. Hardly so! As the "artist," all you have to decide is whether the rock strata will be horizontal or vertical. Rock carving can take place on any type of scenic base. Just plop on plaster and carve!

Here's how I do it. Over the scenic base apply a thick coat of plaster of paris or premixed wallboard joint compound. I like joint compound because I don't have to mix it. It's also inexpensive: I bought a 12-pound tub for $4, and it's even cheaper if you buy a larger tub.

Pre-wet the scenic base so it won't suck the moisture from the plaster and change its setting characteristics. I use a palette knife to swirl on the plaster or joint compound. Apply it thickly enough that there will be some depth left after you get through carving the rock faces.

Texture the wet plaster with a stiff-bristled brush. I use the tip of the brush and texture with a stabbing

The fastest way to shape Styrofoam is with a wire brush mounted in an electric drill. It scrapes away lots of foam quickly, but creates a big mess. Have a vacuum cleaner handy to suck up the bits of foam before they escape.

motion. Or wad up a ball of aluminum foil with a rough surface facing outward and push the ball into the plaster. This leaves a random texture that will be further exaggerated by the carving process. Then allow the plaster to set for several days, until it's hard and dry.

CARVING TECHNIQUES

The carving itself is easy. Using a ½"-wide wood chisel, start at the top (if you want vertical strata) and remove plaster at random. Shave away the plaster, keeping the chisel strokes parallel. Work gently, with just enough pressure on the chisel to remove the plaster—the last thing you

For smoothing and finishing the scenery contours, use a Stanley Surform tool. It makes fine-shaping areas near the edge of the layout or around tunnel portals a snap.

want to do is crack the scenery base.

Every once in a while stop, get a cup of coffee, then return to the layout to view your work. Does it look like rock? If not, add more joint compound or plaster and try again. Practice is important; the more rocks you carve, the better you'll get at it.

If the rocks look okay to you, continue carving. Remember, you only have to please yourself. When you've finished carving, sweep the plaster chips into a bag and save them. (I'll cover coloring rock faces after I discuss how to make rocks with molds.)

MAKING ROCK MOLDS

Rock molds are a good alternative to carving, and making your own molds

Sculptamold is a lightweight scenery material that will adhere to Styrofoam. Spread it over the foam in a thin layer with a spatula.

Smooth and shape the Sculptamold while it is still wet, using a wet nylon brush.

You can carve your own rocks and you don't have to be an artist! Apply a ½"-thick coat of premixed wallboard joint compound over the Sculptamold base. Don't apply too much—it will crack as it dries.

is the best way to get rocks that are unique to your layout. Nowadays, with relatively inexpensive latex molding rubber widely available, more modelers are trying this technique than ever before.

Almost any air-drying molding rubber from your local craft or hobby store will work, but some brands work better than others. I prefer latex rubber (it should say that on the label) to "molding compounds." Latex rubber is easy to apply and can be diluted slightly with water; each layer dries completely overnight. In dry climates latex dries in eight or ten hours. I use rubber latex made by AMACO (American Art Clay Company).

The first step is to select several rocks that have a miniature rock formation on their surface. I've collected more than a dozen while on vacation trips around the country. If trekking though the wild to find likely-looking rocks doesn't turn you on, you can also buy the rock masters. Several companies sell high-impact foam rocks that are sold as mold masters. I've made molds from both Mountains in Minutes and Featherlite brands. Both offer a variety of different rock types.

Set the rock or rock master on your work surface and wash the face with warm soap and water. Remove all loose stone particles, dirt, and debris,

then pat the surface dry with paper towels to remove excess soap. Now give the surface a good squirt of clean water from a plant mister or window sprayer.

While the surface of the rock is wet, apply the first coat of rubber. This is the most important layer, so make sure you get rubber into every crack and seam. I use 1½" and 2" disposable paintbrushes, and I wash the

Carving your own rocks is easy. Use a ½"-wide wood chisel and chip away randomly, working from top to bottom. Hold the chisel so your strokes are parallel and shave away a little at a time.

Making your own rock molds can be a lot of fun. You can use almost any brand of air-drying molding rubber available. AMACO (American Art Clay Company) makes a latex rubber that is available at your local craft or hobby store.

If you can't find a real rock that has the kind of detail you need, try one of the several Polyfoam rocks that are sold as mold masters. Use these just as you would real rocks.

brush with plenty of warm water after each use.

After you've covered the surface of the rock with the first thin layer of rubber, allow it to dry overnight. Apply a second coat of rubber the next day. This layer can be thicker, since the object now is to build up mold thickness and strength.

REINFORCING THE MOLD

To help the mold keep its shape and to prevent the rubber from tearing, add cheesecloth or gauze between the third and fourth applications of rubber. I buy cheesecloth in a fabric store.

You can also use rolled gauze bandages from the drugstore, but they're a lot more expensive. I've also had success using the netlike material of onion bags.

This is a good time to add the fabric reinforcement, because the rock face has been rounded and smoothed by three layers of rubber, and the gauze will lie flat on the surface without creating air pockets. Cut the cheesecloth ahead of time with scissors. I use several long, thin strips rather than one large piece.

Apply a thin coat of rubber, then lay the gauze strips over the rock surface so they overlap. The strips should be wide enough that they overhang the edges of the rock. You can trim them later. Push the gauze into the wet rubber with the tip of your brush, forcing it into all the dips and depressions.

Using a hand sprayer, give the gauze a quick spray to dampen its surface. The water settles the gauze into the rock and slightly thins the next application of rubber. Apply a coat of rubber over the gauze, pushing with the tip of the brush to keep the gauze in contact with the rock. Brush with the "grain" of the gauze so it will lie smooth.

Let the gauze layer of rubber dry thoroughly, then apply two more coats of rubber to smooth and seal the surface. When these dry the mold is done. Carefully peel the mold from the rock, trying not to leave any rubber behind. I trim the edges with heavy scissors to remove excess gauze and rubber. Trim up to, but not into, the area of the mold where the detail begins.

Does this seem like too much work? If so, several manufacturers make ready-to-use rock molds. They make excellent rocks, especially if you make the castings with Polyfoam. But none of the rocks you produce from a store-bought mold will be quite as satisfying as those cast in a mold you make yourself.

CASTING IN THE MOLDS

You make rock castings from plaster, and it really doesn't matter what kind you use. Patching plaster, plaster of paris, and molding plaster all work equally well. The best advice is to buy plaster that is fresh from a supplier who sells a lot of it. If you buy more than 40 pounds, repackage it into smaller portions to keep it dry and fresh; it'll also be easier to handle. I use double plastic food storage bags because I live where it's always damp. Store the packages in a waterproof container with a tight-fitting lid.

Cover your work surface with several thicknesses of newspaper or plastic sheeting. Fill a cardboard box with Styrofoam packing peanuts and set it on the paper. Scoop out a handful of peanuts to make a well for the mold, and place the mold in the box, cavity side up. The mold should sit level, with all of the sides supported by the peanuts.

Spray the mold cavity with wet water. This breaks the surface tension and allows the plaster to flow, bubble free, into all the nooks and crannies in the mold.

REINFORCING THIN CASTINGS

I've tried adding all kinds of reinforcing materials to wet plaster

while it's in the mold. The best I've found is fiberglass joint tape, the stuff that's used with joint compound for plaster board or drywall construction. It comes in several widths; I use 3" wide. Cut a piece a little smaller than the mold and push it into the wet plaster, but not so far that it touches the face of the mold.

Start making the mold by washing the rock face with soap and warm water to remove any dirt. While the rock is wet, apply the first coat of rubber.

Mixing and pouring plaster

The trick to mixing plaster properly, if there is one, is to always add plaster to water. Pour 1 cup cold water in a plastic container with a smooth bottom, then gradually sprinkle 1 cup plaster into it. The plaster will dissolve into the water as it hits the surface. After all the plaster is dissolved, stir it for several minutes to mix completely. Tap the bottom of the container to remove trapped air bubbles. The stirring will add a few bubbles, but this can't be helped.

Slowly pour the plaster into the mold. Tap and shake the mold to remove air bubbles that could mar the surface of the casting. If the plaster doesn't quite fill the mold, pick it up and swirl the plaster until it coats all the surfaces, all the way to the rim of the mold. Continue swirling until the plaster starts to set. As it thickens you can change the swirling to a gentle tilting of the mold. Tilt it round and round until the plaster no longer will flow. Now place it down and let it set. Later you can fill the rest of the mold with a fresh batch of plaster—or use the casting hollow.

After you've applied three thick coats of rubber and they have dried, it's time to reinforce the mold. Add a layer of cheesecloth or gauze and seal it in place with several additional applications of rubber.

Slowly peel the mold from the rock, being careful not to tear it. The cheesecloth reinforcement makes a good handle.

The joint tape helps hold the casting together. This is important if the mold is so deeply undercut and angular that the casting gets stuck. Occasionally I crack thin castings intentionally to conform to the shape of the underlying terrain. With the tape inside, the casting holds together and allows me to fit it to the scenery base.

PLASTIC FOAM FOR SCENERY

Polyfoam, a two-part expanding urethane plastic foam, is an alternative to plaster for molding rocks. The most common product offered for hobby use is Mountains in Minutes Polyfoam, parts A and B.

You'll also need a mold release, which keeps the foam from sticking to your mold and ruining it. I've tried several mold-release agents, only to be convinced that the best one always come from the foam manufacturer. So look for Mountains in Minutes Mold Release Concentrate; in a pinch you can substitute Scotch Guard fabric protector in the spray can.

The foam expands several times as it cures, and it pushes toward the path of least resistance. To keep the foam in the mold I use an 18" square of ½" plywood, a cement block for weight, and a sheet of plastic film large enough to cover the mold.

To mix the two parts I use 10-ounce

You can use the mold you just made to cast rocks directly onto the layout. Fill the mold with plaster and tap the bottom to remove any air bubbles. As the plaster starts to set, place the mold on the scenery. Hold it in place until the mold gets warm, then gently peel the mold from the casting.

paper coffee cups and wooden tongue depressors. Cut one end of each tongue depressor square—this makes it easier to scrape out the bottom of the cup. Wear a pair of disposable latex examination gloves while mixing and pouring to keep the Polyfoam off your hands. Be careful with Polyfoam because it sticks to everything and is very hard to remove.

MAKING POLYFOAM ROCKS

Here I'll explain how to cast Polyfoam rocks on the workbench, paint them, then install them on the layout. You can also make the castings directly on the layout, but I'll explain that later.

Start by covering your bench with a sheet of plastic. (A trash bag, slit up one side and along the bottom, works well.) Give the inside of the mold a good coating of mold release and let it dry for several minutes.

Measure equal parts of A and B Polyfoam, each in its own cup. Pour part A into B, scrape the sides of the A cup to get it all, and mix until the

Another way to make rock castings is with Mountains in Minutes Polyfoam. These polyurethane castings can be made on the workbench. They are lightweight and easy to paint.

Prepare the mold by spraying it with a mold release. If the release wets the surface of the mold, wait until it dries before proceeding.

Mix equal parts of A and B Polyfoam and drizzle it into the mold. Add enough to cover about half the bottom of the mold. Estimating how much foam to mix and use is the only tricky part of the casting process. Too much foam and you have waste, too little and the mold will only be partially filled.

color is uniform. Knowing how much to mix takes a little practice. Start by following the manufacturer's instructions, then adjust the amount to suit your mold.

Drizzle the foam into the mold, covering about half the bottom. There's no need to cover the bottom of the mold completely, because the foam will expand to about 20 times its volume. As the foam starts to expand, cover the mold with a sheet of plastic, place the plywood on top, and weight it with the cement block.

Adjust the block so that it sits level on the plywood.

It takes about 20 minutes for the foam to expand to fill the mold, cure, and cool. Do not disturb the mold until it is cool to the touch. The foam will remain slightly sticky until it cures completely.

To remove the casting, start at one corner and peel the mold away, being careful not to rip the mold or break the Polyfoam. If the mold has deep undercuts or trapped air bubbles some tearing will be unavoidable.

To prepare the mold for another casting, pick out all the small bits of foam clinging to the surface. If some stick stubbornly, rub the area with the palm of your hand. Rub until all the foam is gone, then spray on another coat of mold release and repeat the above steps.

TRIMMING POLYFOAM CASTINGS

Because you can't control the flow of the Polyfoam as it expands, the castings will have thick and thin areas. I remove excess thickness from the back of the castings with a hacksaw blade, handsaw, or bandsaw. To use the

The foam will expand to about 20 times its volume, filling the mold. The expansion has to be contained to force the expanding foam into the mold.

hacksaw blade or handsaw I place the casting face down on the workbench and trim off unwanted portions, holding the blade parallel to the workbench top.

For larger castings I prefer the band saw. It's fast and precise, and produces the least waste. I raise the saw guard as high as it will go, stand the casting on end, and slice away. Be sure to wear a dust respirator and keep your fingers away from the blade.

COLORING POLYFOAM CASTINGS

It's hard to tell exactly how good the casting is until you paint it. I prepaint the raw rocks so I can see the detail. After the rock is placed on the layout there will be places that can't be reached with brush or spray, so prepainting makes sure that all the hard-to-reach spots are colored.

Set all the castings you've made on a large sheet of newspaper and spray

As the foam starts to expand, cover the mold with a sheet of plastic. The foam won't stick to the plastic, so it can be removed easily.

Next, place a sheet of plywood on top of the plastic and add a cement block for weight. The weight forces the foam to expand into the mold, filling all nooks and crannies.

After about 20 minutes remove the casting from the mold. Starting at one corner, carefully peel the mold away from the casting. Try not to rip the mold or break the casting, which is still slightly sticky.

them from all four directions with a light coat of Floquil engine black. If you use other brands, test them on scrap foam to make sure they're compatible. Some paints contain solvents that will craze or melt foam.

The black gets in all the nooks and crannies and creates artificial shadows. Allow the black to dry for an hour, then spray on Floquil earth from one direction only. This creates the rock color and provides highlights. These two colors give the castings enough relief so you can get all the rock strata on the same plane. You'll finish painting after the castings are in place on the layout.

INSTALLING POLYFOAM ROCKS

I never use the complete castings as they come from the mold. They're always too big, even for a tinplate layout, so I snap them along their natural seams to make smaller rocks. I can then cut them and shape them with a small knife or hacksaw blade so they'll fit together and conform to the terrain.

Install the rocks by starting at the bottom of the hill and working up, stacking the castings to assemble a realistic rock face. Fasten the castings in place with Liquid Nails from the caulking gun. A little dab of adhesive on the back of each piece is enough to hold it in position.

As gap fillers, use the small scraps that you trimmed from the castings to make them fit together. Glue them between the larger pieces to fill voids. There will still be plenty of voids and places where the flat back of the casting doesn't quite fit the contour of the scenic base; you'll fix them next.

FINISHING AROUND THE ROCKS

Wait overnight for the Liquid Nails to set. Once the rocks are held securely to the scenic base, it's time to

To trim the castings, use a band saw. Slice them down the middle to remove excess thickness, then trim the sides so they'll fit in a given area. You can also use a handsaw for this purpose.

bring the scenic contours up to the edges of the castings and then finish painting them.

Using Sculptamold mixed with water and a stiff 3" nylon brush, blend the edges of the castings into the existing scenic contours. Brush Sculptamold from the scenic base toward the castings to fill any gaps or hollows. Wet the brush in clean water and continue smoothing until the castings look as if they grew out of the base.

Allow the Sculptamold to set up (about 15 minutes) and spray the rocks with a black wash made by adding a tablespoon of acrylic black or india ink to a pint of water. Add several drops of detergent as well. Allow the black wash to dry for several hours. All you have to do now is lighten the rock

At the layout the molds are cut to fit together on the rock slope jigsaw-puzzle fashion.

Prepaint the rocks before they're set in place on the layout. Then you'll get paint into all the hard-to-reach places that you won't be able to reach later. Use two colors: flat black and Floquil earth, both in a spray can.

The advantage to using rock casting in small pieces is that you can arrange them to conform to almost any terrain. Hold the castings in place with a dab of Liquid Nails.

The scrap castings were used inside this tunnel. After they were all set in place the interior of the tunnel was sprayed lightly with flat black paint, then drybrushed to bring out the detail.

color and drybrush the outer surfaces.

Dilute about a cup of earth-color latex paint with three cups of water, and add about a tablespoon of any water-based black acrylic paint. I've used acrylic artist's colors, Polly S, universal tinting colors, and india ink. All will darken the earth color.

With a wide, flat brush, sparingly dab this mixture onto the upper surfaces of the rocks. This gives the castings a uniform coloring that blends with the other earth tones on the layout. If there are areas where the honey color of the raw foam still shows, touch them up now. Allow the earth color to dry.

Drybrushing is the last step. You'll need flat white paint, a pad of paper

towels, and a large, soft brush. Pick up a little paint on the tip of the brush and wipe most of it off on the paper

Complex rock faces can be crafted from many small castings made from just one mold. The castings were cut and stacked to fit around the tunnel portal, then lightly sprayed with a black wash.

Here's the first step in coloring the hand-carved rocks. Dilute 1 cup earth-color latex paint with 3 cups water, and add 1 tablespoon black acrylic paint. Spray the paint on the rock with a pump-type plant mister.

Finish coloring the rock face by flowing on a wash of water and burnt sienna acrylic color. After the wash dries, dry-brush the rock face with Polly S reefer white paint on a wide brush.

more detail than there actually is. Be careful, though—too much scrubbing will make the rocks look as if they're covered with frost.

FINISHING WITH FOAM PUTTY

To fill between the rocks I make what I call "foam putty"—a mixture of green scenic foam and dilute white glue (three parts water to one part glue). Put some foam (there are no exact proportions) in a shallow dish and add enough dilute glue to make a paste the consistency of cooked rice. If you squeeze the mixture between your fingers it should release only a few drops of white glue. Experiment with the consistency; you may like it wetter.

I wear a pair of latex gloves to keep my fingers clean while using the putty. Grab a lump of the mixture and, starting at the bottom of the rock face, push it around the edges of the rocks. The idea is to add the foam everywhere there's a gap, seam, or mismatch between the castings. Push the putty into place, trying not to smooth it—it should look rough and

towels. There should only be enough paint left on the brush to leave a hint of white when it's wiped over the casting's surface. Start at the top of the rock face and lightly brush downward.

As the brush gradually becomes loaded with almost-dry paint, you can scrub the castings with it. This works best on rocks that have little or no detail. The scrubbing lightens every rise on the rock surface, no matter how small, and gives the illusion of

Use foam putty to finish around the castings and to make them look as though they "popped" from the hillside. This is a mixture of green scenic foam and dilute white glue, mixed together in a shallow dish to make an oatmeal-like paste.

The finished rocks are very understated in this completed scene. They should look as if they're just poking their noses through the underbrush. The earth and black coloring mixture and the drybrushing produce realistic results.

ragged like scrubby growth. Keep adding foam putty until all the rock faces are completely surrounded. When you add ground cover later it will blend into the foam-puttied gaps, making a seamless transition.

Filling gaps around rocks isn't the only use for foam putty. I use it wherever I need the look of low, ragged growth or hanging vines. It's especially useful for hiding the edges of tunnel portals, the gaps where bridges meet the scenery, and the seam along the backdrop. I like to use different shades of green around a rock face to add color and variety. I keep several colors of foam putty in plastic Zip-Loc sandwich bags.

Toolbox of equipment

To make Styrofoam hills and mountains:
- ✓ Serrated-edge knife
- ✓ Hacksaw blade
- ✓ Foam-compatible adhesive
- ✓ Caulking gun
- ✓ Surform tool
- ✓ Large, soft-bristled paint brush

To make plaster rocks:
- ✓ Large, stiff-bristled paint brush
- ✓ Aluminum foil
- ✓ ½" wood chisel

To cast and install Polyfoam rocks:
- ✓ 16-ounce plant sprayer
- ✓ Disposable foam brush
- ✓ Disposable cups
- ✓ Wooden tongue depressor
- ✓ Disposable latex gloves
- ✓ Hacksaw blade
- ✓ Foam-compatible adhesive
- ✓ Caulking gun
- ✓ Large, stiff-bristled brush
- ✓ Large, soft-bristled brush

Roads on a model railroad are the single most powerful way to tie structures and scenery together. Roads can be scene dividers, as well. And they can be a powerful way to force perspective to make your layout look larger than it really is.

5 Building Roads

The roads on your model railroad are links that connect cities and factories and farms. Because they're also important visual elements, give some thought to where they'll go and what they'll connect.

WHERE TO PUT ROADS

Before I get out my road-building materials, I spend a lot of time moving structures around the layout to see where they look best. Once I have the buildings where they will serve the railroad best, I draw the connecting roads with a wide felt-tip marker. It's important to leave enough space for parking lots, loading and unloading facilities, and turning areas for trucks. Your roads can be almost any width— as long as two model trucks can pass

Build the road base from ¼"-thick foam-core board glued to the base with white glue or Liquid Nails. The weights hold the road flat until the glue dries.

To make a dirt road, apply earth-color latex paint over the foam core. If the paint seems thin, brush on a second coat of paint to seal the foam core.

each other, or look as though they can.

Roads are also useful as scene dividers. They create realistic quiet areas between the structures and scenic elements. Best of all, they can be a powerful way to help you force perspective and make your layout look larger than it really is. All roads that run toward the background should become narrower as they recede from the viewer. Curved and "S"-shaped roads that also narrow are twice as effective as straight ones.

Another space-expanding technique is to run the roads off the edge of the layout, only to have them re-enter the layout across the aisle or on the other side of the mountain.

This is a tea strainer. It has a very fine stainless-steel mesh at the bottom and makes a great sifter for adding very fine sand to road surfaces.

several layers of shirt cardboard, all with similar results.

Foam core is the same material I used to make the ties. Its thickness brings the road even with the tops of the Lionel metal ties; if I need more height, I stack another layer of foam core to make a thicker road and to bring it to the top of the rail.

Cutting foam core is easy for straight roads. All you need is a carpenter's square and a hobby knife with a new blade. Mark the road width on the foam core, then cut, holding the knife blade tightly against the square to keep the paper from tearing.

Lay the road pieces on the layout and cut the ends, using the square, so they will all fit together. Don't worry about the seams; they'll be covered with paint and texture. I like to use either white glue or Liquid Nails to fasten the road sections in place. After applying the glue and putting the sections back in position, place weights on each end and at the seams until the glue dries.

Now that the planning is complete, you have to decide what type of road to build. The two types most commonly modeled are dirt roads and asphalt (or hot-top) roads. The basic construction for both roads starts with the same materials—only the finishing differs.

Nowadays, I like to build the road base from ¼" thick foam-core board. I've also used corrugated cardboard or

Fill the tea strainer with contractor's sand and sprinkle it into the wet paint. Shake it up to and slightly over the edge of the road. Work in sections, each overlapping the last, until the road is finished.

The stones remaining in the strainer make great detail along the edge of the roads. Just sprinkle the small stones in place, wet with water, and drizzle on dilute white glue.

You can add fine sand texture anywhere. Just mix together glue and fine sand to make a thick paint. Use this mixture to make a dirt road where none existed before. Here, it's covering a roadside embankment.

In preparation for making the tar road, use fine gravel to bring the grade up to the track level.

For the tar road mix equal parts of flat black paint and earth-color paint. Brush it over the foam core and then sprinkle fine sand through the tea strainer. After the paint dries, apply another coat of black to seal the surface.

Curved roads take a little more work. You have to guess where to cut the curves, and you have to cut them freehand, without the aid of a straight-edge. Take a piece of foam core to the layout, set it over the area where the road curves, and sketch the shape. Using a hobby knife, cut a little outside the lines. Then replace the road piece on the layout and trim to fit.

Roads that go uphill take more work yet, because foam core doesn't like to bend—it creases when bent. I cut a lot of narrow strips that are the width of the road and I glue them down like tiles, adjusting each strip to the grade. The numerous seams will be smoothed out as the road surface is painted and textured.

BUILD A DIRT ROAD

Gather the materials you'll need: dirt-colored latex paint, the same earth-tone paint as for the rest of the layout, some sort of sifter, and a fine texture. The sifter I like best is called a tea strainer. It's a small cup with a fine screen on the bottom and a handle.

I found mine in the kitchen section of a housewares store. You can also use a piece of nylon stocking or pantyhose stretched over a wire hoop.

The road's surface texture can be the fine rock powder sold for model landscaping, real dirt from your yard (dry it and remove any large pieces), contractor's sand (sold in bags for mixing with cement), or baseball diamond dressing. In fact, you can use just about any fine texture, as long as it's a light color.

If you select contractor's sand, sift it through several screens with different-sized mesh to remove the large stones. Use the finest grade for roads. The baseball diamond dressing is a fine, clay-based compound sold just for topping baseball infields. I gathered some of this material at a little league field. When I accumulate a coffee can full of this compound, I dry it on newspaper and store it plastic sandwich bags. It can be used as is.

Spread a thick coat of full-strength earth-color latex paint over the foam-core base. While the paint is still wet,

Blend the edges of the road into the rest of the scenery before the road is weathered. Sprinkle grass and dead-leaf-colored foam, then sprinkle it with dilute white glue to hold it in place. Weather the road when the glue dries.

The first step in weathering the road is to apply a light dusting of dirt-colored pastel chalk. Grind the chalk on a sheet of sandpaper and store it in a 35mm film can. Apply it with a soft, wide brush, brushing in the direction of the road.

A fine-tipped black marker makes great-looking cracks and tar lines on the road. You can let your imagination run wild and add as many lines as you want, and the road will still look prototypical.

sprinkle on enough texture, through the tea strainer or stocking, to cover the wet paint. Sprinkle it up to and slightly over the edge of the road. Work in sections, each overlapping the last, until the road is finished. Let the road dry overnight.

The next day, vacuum loose texture from the road surface and apply another layer of earth paint—only this time dilute the paint with equal parts of water. Again sprinkle a light coating of texture into the paint. This extra texture gives the road a rough look. Allow the paint to set for about 30 minutes; then you can add ruts or wheel marks. Use a pencil, screwdriver tip, or modeling knife, and lightly draw the tool toward you in parallel strokes, or roll a model car along the road. (Don't forget to wash the paint from the wheels.)

After the road is dry, weather it by lightly drybrushing its surface with flat white paint. For a real backwoods look brush the road surface with earth-tone powdered chalks to vary the color.

Another way to model the fine-textured surface of a dirt road, wooded paths, cattle trails, and sand embankments, is to make sand paint. Mix together dilute white glue and the fine sand produced by sifting contractor's sand or baseball diamond clay through the tea strainer.

Brush this mixture everywhere you want to model fine texture. Use it over scenic foam and along the sides of the road. Sprinkle scenic foam, twigs, leaves, and flocking over it for extra texture.

ASPHALT MADE EASY

To build the tar road, start by mixing equal parts of flat black latex paint and earth-color latex paint. Brush it over the foam-core surface and sprinkle on the fine texture. After the paint dries, apply a second coat of the black-and-earth paint to seal in the texture.

When the paint dries add cracks and tar repairs to the tar road with a fine-tipped black marker. Paint traffic lines in the center of the road by making a stencil from a sheet of cardboard with a long rectangular slit cut in it. Hold the stencil over the center of the road and lightly spray with Floquil reefer yellow. Weather the road by drybrushing with white to bring out the surface texture, and dust along the edges with earth-color pastel chalk.

A light drybrushing with white will bring out the surface texture of the road. Here simple details have been added up to the edge of the road to blend it into the scenery.

Toolbox of equipment

To build roads:
✓ Straightedge
✓ Carpenter's square
✓ Black permanent marker
✓ Hobby knife
✓ White glue
✓ Tea strainer
✓ Large, soft-bristled paintbrush

Lots of trees help make the scene look realistic. Only three different types of trees make up this very convincing forest.

6 Planting Trees

No scenic element adds realism to scenery as trees do. They can be almost any size or shape or construction quality. The magic happens when you group all the different types of trees together into a forest. When you use all the types together, you only notice the beauty of the setting, not the individual trees. To create the forests for your tinplate layouts you're going to need a lot of trees—so start with the easiest.

MAKING WEED TREES

Trees based on weeds are the easiest to make, as well as the least expensive. All sorts of tree-shaped weeds, dried flower stalks, and woody branches are available, depending on where you live. As a rule of thumb, the

Except for the pine trees, this forest was made from weeds picked in the fields. Dip each weed in a different color of scenic foam for variety.

best time to look for them is after the first frost, when most plants have shed their leaves.

Modelers in the desert areas of the southwestern United States have an especially plentiful supply of tree-making materials. The favorite for tinplate modelers is sagebrush: Its woody branches make excellent trees when covered with fine scenery netting and scenic foam.

Start by gathering tree-shaped weeds. Stand each one upright in a sheet of Styrofoam. If the bark is loose or flaky, cement it by dipping the weed structure in dilute white glue (three parts water to one part glue). Add a few drops of dishwashing detergent to the water to help it flow into all the cracks and crevices of the bark. Let the weed soak until the glue and water have been absorbed (the bark will charge color), remove, shake away excess liquid, and stand it in the foam to dry. Paint the bark if necessary, following the steps described below for coloring the trunks of commercial trees.

ADDING FOLIAGE

The dip method. The first way to add foliage is to dip the weed branches

Use tree-shaped weeds and dried flower stalks to make easy, inexpensive trees. These are sumac tips picked in the desert of southern California. They're not related to the sumac plants found in the northern states.

into the dilute glue mixture, shake off excess glue, and plunge the branches into scenic foam. You can make this foam mixture from any extra tree-green colors you have on hand, or you can blend the colors with a specific season in mind.

I make the foam mixture by tossing several bags of coarse medium-green scenic foam into a plastic grocery bag. Coarse-textured foam is ideal: It fills in between the branches and looks good on just about any sort of tree armature. Add a bag or two of yellow-green, a bag of brown, and a bag of dark green to the coarse foam. If

These weed trees are the woody branches of a blueberry bush, dipped in dilute white glue and plunged in a bag of coarse green foam.

tree kits. You cover the branch structure with fine netting, then cover that with ground foam, punched paper bits, or dyed sawdust.

If you start with a tree kit, follow the instructions and use the materials provided. I usually build tree kits in front of the TV while watching a ball game. Neither task requires your complete attention, so you can have a relaxing evening and produce some trees to boot!

Start the kit trees by bending the branches to shape, then set each armature aside for painting. Vary the shape from tree to tree; most of them will be placed in groups, so you don't have to make every one perfect. In fact, odd-shaped trees, especially ones with flat or cupped sides, sometimes fit better with other trees.

Stand the armatures on a Styrofoam block and spray them with flat brown or gray paint. Glue very large trees to individual cardboard squares for easier handling. After the paint dries, drybrush the bark near the bottom of the trunk to bring out the texture.

I use Woodland Scenics FP178 Poly Fiber for the branch structure that will eventually hold the leaves. This is a puffy green fiber material, the same product sold in fabric stores (in white only) as pillow stuffing. A bag will make about seven medium-sized O scale trees.

Whether you build from a kit or from scratch, you'll need glue to hold the netting to the branches. I use Aleene's Original tacky glue, sold in hobby, craft, hardware, and department stores. This thick acrylic white glue holds fast and dries in minutes. Unlike regular white glue, tacky glue has enough body to stay where you put it.

You'll also need a can of spray glue. I use both 3M Super 77 spray adhesive and super-hold hair spray. The spray glue holds the netting to itself and glues the leaf texture to the netting.

Tear off three or four pieces of the Poly Fiber and glue them to the tops

you're modeling autumn, mix a dead-leaf brown, several yellows, and yellow-red or orange. When your tree-making sessions are over, save any extra foam mixture to use as a matching ground texture and to make foam putty.

Using fiber netting. The second tree-making technique is more complex. It's the technique used in most

Spray the foliage netting with glue or super-hold hair spray and sprinkle on fine green scenic foam and Noch green paper flocking. Add only enough leaf texture to achieve a wispy, see-through look. The same techniques can be used on a large weed.

of the main branch structure with several drops of tacky glue.

Now tear several more pieces of Poly Fiber away from the main bundle. Pull and stretch until each piece is large and fluffy, like a cloud. Make enough of these little clouds to build several trees at once.

Spray the Poly Fiber that's already on the tree armature with spray glue, then add the cloudlike pieces to the top and sides of the tree. You don't have to make the tree symmetrical— odd shapes are better. The last thing you want is a bunch of trees that look like fuzzy lollipops.

Now spray all the foliage with glue and sprinkle on fine green ground foam or paper bits. Apply only enough leaf texture to achieve a wispy, see-through look; if you add too much the tree will look solid. I sprinkle the darker-colored textures on the lower parts of the tree, saving the lighter colors for the top.

SPRUCING UP COMMERCIAL TREES

The easiest way to add great-looking trees to your layout is to improve store-bought products. Prices vary

A commercially available weed product called Filgrunebaum, sold by Scenic Express, made these fine-looking weed trees. Just spray the Filgrunebaum with hair spray or dilute glue and sprinkle it with paper flocking.

widely, and your best bet is to choose several brands in different price ranges. Buy the more expensive and detailed trees to use in the foreground of your layout, and choose inexpensive bottle-brush or "fuzzy lollipop" trees for the background. With a little work they will rival the best handmade trees.

Background trees can be any scale, as long as they are smaller than those in the foreground, so you can use inexpensive trees intended for HO or N scale in the background of your

Always look for bargain trees when you visit the hobby shop. They can usually be spruced up to make them acceptable.

First trim this funny-looking specimen to shape, then spray the foliage with forest green. While the paint is wet, sprinkle on fine dark green foam to model the pine needles.

Spray the trunk with flat brown automotive primer. A little overspray is okay on the under-branches—it will make them look dead.

Finish the trunk by drybrushing the cast bark texture with off-white. Make an ivory color by mixing a little acrylic brown with white.

Look how the spruced-up tree compares with a more expensive store-bought tree! Highlight the outer branches with a medium green spray. The tree behind it is only a half tree, glued directly to the backdrop.

tinplate layout. The trick is simple: Always place the smaller trees behind the larger ones.

No matter what size the trees are, stand them upright on a large sheet of Styrofoam or cardboard. Hold trees with wide cast bases in place with a drop of white glue, and push those without bases into the foam.

I like to paint the trunks realistic colors. There are two ways to approach this. The first is to spray the trunks flat brown. Grasp a tree by its top, hold it over newspaper, and spray the trunk while twirling the tree. A little overspray on the bottom branches is okay—it won't be visible after you apply the foliage.

The second technique is to brush the trunks with flat brown acrylic paint. Hold the tree by the tip and paint the trunk top to bottom, then stick each painted tree back in the Styrofoam base to dry.

Finish coloring the trunks by highlighting the bark texture. Pour flat gray acrylic paint into a shallow dish, and wet the tip of a soft, wide brush (like the ones used to paint structures) in the paint. Wipe off most of the paint, then whisk the tip of the brush lightly over the trunk from top to bottom. You want to deposit paint only on the raised portions of the bark. Don't overdo it—a little drybrushing goes a long way.

Next, trim the foliage to shape with scissors. Pine trees seem to need this step more than leafy trees. Some of the

This pine tree kit is very easy to build. Even though these trees are HO scale, they make perfect background trees for O scale. Twist the plastic trunks into a pine tree shape and spray them with dark brown paint. Apply the glue to the bottom branches and add the foliage.

Here's a completed tree. The foliage is made from chunks of Woodland Scenics FC58 medium green foliage clusters glued to the branches. The tree now needs only a little trimming with scissors and it's ready for the layout.

Make the background trees from golf-ball sized balls of Poly Fiber. Stretch it into pieces, then tear away enough to make a ball. Drop each ball into a small bowl of thinned white glue, then roll it in scenic foam.

on a very fine medium green foam while the paint is wet. After the paint dries more shaping may be necessary

A good way to give a tree an old, ratty look, is to run the foliage through your fist several times, knocking off some of the texture. Work over a sheet of newspaper so you can catch the foam and reuse it.

COMMERCIAL PINE TREE KITS

Several manufacturers sell kits to make pine trees. I like the kits that use a plastic trunk with short, stubby, spikelike branches. Simply cover them with a dark green clumpy foliage material, and you'll have good-looking trees very quickly.

Using two pairs of pliers, twist the plastic trunks about five times, or until all the branches are radial. Then tack them to a Styrofoam base for painting. I spray them with dark brown paint.

After the paint dries, remove each tree from the base to apply the foliage. Start on the bottom branches and brush a layer of Aleene's tacky glue or Woodland Scenics Hob-e-Tac adhesive.

trees have wire branches, so this step is more hacking then cutting, but remove enough to change the shape of the tree and make it more, or less, symmetrical. After trimming I spray the pine foliage dark green and sprinkle

Glue the finished balls to the distant hills, using full-strength white glue. Pack them as tightly as possible so they look like treetops.

It's easy to make hundreds of little pine trees to use on the background hills. Pull apart nylon scouring pads and cut them into small triangular pieces. They are porous when held up to the light but take on a solid look when coated in dark green foam.

These glues are both very sticky and will hold the foliage in place until they dry. Aleene's tacky glue is a thick white glue, and Hob-e-Tac is a cross between airplane and rubber cement, although it never seems to dry completely. It will hold the weight of the clump foliage while the tree is tipped and handled.

Impale a small chunk of Woodland Scenics FC58 medium green foliage clusters onto each branch. Rip up several dozen pieces before starting a tree, and just push them on the branches. Use the larger chunks at the bottom and the smaller pieces at the top of the tree.

To finish each tree, spray-paint with medium green, holding the can over the top of the tree and spraying straight down. Try not to spray the trunk. This lighter color highlights the outer branches, achieving the same effect as drybrushing.

BACKGROUND DECIDUOUS TREES

Unless you're modeling the desert or the face of the moon, you'll need a lot

Several manufacturers offer small bottle-brush trees. They are inexpensive, so you get a lot for your money. To improve the looks of these trees, coat them with fine, dark green texture.

You can make another quick background tree from the branches of an old artificial Christmas tree. Cut them to size and shape, trim off the bottom branches, and cover with green foam.

of small background trees to cover a hillside or mountain. The easiest way I've found is to use Woodland Scenics FP178 Poly Fiber covered with the same scenic foam mixture used to make weed trees.

Stretch the Poly Fiber into thin layers, then tear away enough fiber to make fluffy balls a little larger than golf balls. I wear latex gloves to keep my hands clean, and to help me hold the fiber. Drop each ball into a small bowl of thinned white glue (three parts water to one part glue).

When the bowl is filled, grab a handful of foam balls, squeeze out the excess glue, and drop them into a tray containing mixed green scenic foam. Toss the balls until they're completely coated with foam, shake away excess foam, and set on them on a plastic bag or waxed paper to dry overnight.

Vary the colors of the foam-covered balls by adding a new color as you begin each new batch. This alters the overall color slightly, and as you make a lot of Poly Fiber balls the overall color will change considerably.

When all the batches of foam balls are dry, mix them together in a plastic bag. This will give you a random and realistic variation in the colors. Glue the balls to background hills and mountains using a 50:50 solution of white glue and water. Use paper towels to absorb any excess white glue that runs down the mountain, or sop it up by sprinkling on more scenic foam.

Put the smaller balls in the rear, and use the larger ones toward the front. Pack them in tight so they'll look like a million treetops. To make large tree balls smaller, and to make them go twice as far, cut them in half with large scissors and plant them flat side down.

I add small pine trees, clumps of Woodland Scenics foliage clusters, and

Used together with the Poly Fiber balls, the little pine trees give the mountaintop a vertical dimension that's hard to achieve otherwise.

twigs between the balls after the glue has dried. This varies the uniform bumpy texture, and breaks up the carpet-like appearance.

BACKGROUND PINE TREES

Dozens of pointed little pine trees sticking up between the round-top deciduous trees will give life and definition to your background scenery. Background pine trees are easy to make, and they, too, can be made in front of the TV.

One variety is easy to make from triangular pieces of nylon scouring pads. I use dark brown pads that are about ¾" thick and are porous enough to see through when held up to the light. Start by cutting the pad in half lengthwise using a thin, serrated-blade kitchen knife.

Cut each half into long thin triangles with scissors. Fluff the triangles with your fingers to make them round, and pull any scraps from the pad into thin, wispy pieces. Save these to make weeds.

Dip each pine tree in thinned white glue, shake off excess, and plunge the tree into a shallow tray containing fine-textured dark green foam. Shake again, then stand each tree upright in a block of Styrofoam until the glue dries.

IMPROVING BOTTLE-BRUSH TREES

You can make more background pines by modifying those shiny bottle-brush trees that are sold for small scale layouts. The main problems with these trees are that they all have the same shape and the color is usually bright green.

The individual branches are small, shiny, hair-sized nylon threads. If you cover them with a fine, dark green texture, they'll rival even the best foreground trees. Proceed as described above, dipping each tree in glue, then in fine scenic foam. Look for a foam

Leftover nylon scrubbing pad material makes great tree profiles that hide the edge of the forest. Cut thin pieces of nylon to shape on the bottom and pull them apart to make a random top.

After coating the scouring pads in green foam, glue them in front of the poly balls to look like another type of bush.

Loofah sponges make good background pine trees. These sponges are the dried remains of a large cucumber-like vegetable grown in Asia. They're sold as bath sponges for smoothing rough skin.

After coloring the sponge in fabric dye, remove the core, using a fillet knife with a long, thin blade. This center core is the part of the sponge you'll use to make the tree.

color that closely resembles the color of the pines in the area you're modeling.

BACKGROUND TREE SILHOUETTES

Even the simplest trees are time-consuming to make, and there are situations in which you only need the effect of trees in the background. I wanted to make some separation between the background and the tree balls, especially where I had applied foam putty to make textured background hills. It turned out that left-over nylon scrubbing pad material filled the bill and allowed me to quickly make enough textured tree profiles for a whole layout.

I ripped the nylon pads, lengthwise, into several thin rectangles. Then I pulled and ripped these rectangles into about a dozen pieces with flat bottoms and ragged tops. Grabbing each by the bottom, I dipped it into the glue and rolled it in a tray of scenic foam. Then I set it on a plastic bag so it would dry without sticking to anything.

Later I trimmed the treetops to

Here's the core of the sponge sliced into wafers, each of which is a different size. Push the wafers over the trunk, starting with the largest wafer at the bottom. Make the trunk from a piece of tapered wood covered with crepe-paper bark.

Two different-sized loofah sponge trees are in place on this layout. You can make the trees any size, depending on the size of the sponge.

varying heights and glued the finished sections about ¼" in front of the tree balls. These silhouettes provided a different shape in front of the round balls.

LOOFAH SPONGE PINE TREES

Loofah sponges are the dried remains of a large cucumberlike vegetable grown in Asia. They're sold in drug, health and department stores as bath sponges, and they've been used for centuries to gently scrub away rough skin. When one fell apart I discovered its weblike interior. By cutting it apart further I found it would make a good model pine. (Unknown to me, until I visited a friend who is a tinplate collector, Lionel used loofah sponges to make pine trees for prebuilt scenery displays they sold in the 1930s.)

As it comes from the package the sponge is a straw tan color, which is okay for briar patches and weeds. But because I wanted to make pine trees, my first experiment was to color the loofah sponge green. After bringing 2 quarts of water to a boil in an old saucepan, I added 3 tablespoons of green powdered fabric dye (any dark green shade of Rit or Tintex seems to produce about the right color), and stirred for two or three minutes. When the dye had dissolved completely, I tossed in the sponge and

The leftover pieces of sponge provide a lot of interesting texture. Shred them and use them as weeds and bushes.

submerged it for several minutes. The loofah is very porous, so it absorbs the dye completely.

To remove the sponge from the dye I stuck a long screwdriver into one of the holes in the middle. This allowed me to pick it up, turn it, and drain it without burning my fingers—or turning them green. Hold the sponge over the pot to drain, then place it on several thicknesses of newspaper to dry

Roll a scrap piece of sponge into a tight cone and dip it in glue, then foam, to make a small shrub.

Make these small birch trees by bundling together pieces of pepper grass, brush-painting the trunks, then spray-painting leaves a yellow-green color. Pepper grass is available in craft and hobby stores.

overnight. It's easy to dye several loofah sponges at the same time—one batch of dye will color about three large ones before you have to replenish it with more dye powder.

The core of the loofah is the part to use for pine trees. Remove the center using a fillet knife with a long, thin blade. Run the knife into one of the larger holes and cut around the core in a circular motion until the center comes free as one long cylinder. If you don't have a long thin knife, slice the sponge crosswise into pieces with a serrated bread knife. Cut sections as long as your knife blade, then remove the center from each section.

Next slice the core into thin wafers with the serrated knife. These wafers will become the foliage layers of your tree. A large sponge will make about three trees, so sort the wafers into three equal piles. The largest wafers are used on the bottom, where the tree is widest. The smaller wafers are placed in the middle, tapering to the smallest at the top. Make the tip section at the very top of the tree by trimming the wafers into irregular shapes with scissors.

Add the foliage—or "pine needles"—before positioning the wafers on the trunks. Dip each wafer in a dilute solution of white glue and water (3:1).

Shake off the excess glue before rolling each wafer in fine-textured forest green scenic foam or fine blue-green sawdust. Place the wafers on waxed paper to dry overnight.

Make trunks from ⅜" dowel. Cut them to various lengths, and taper each trunk from top to bottom with coarse sandpaper. On some trunks I wire-brush the lower third and upper tip to make bark texture.

Force a 1" wire brad into base of each trunk, then snip off the head. Then stand the trunks in a Styrofoam block and paint them with a base coat of Polly S roof brown and reefer gray. I mix the colors directly on the trunk, using more gray than brown and streaking the colors from top to bottom.

After the paint dries, give all the trunks a wash of india ink and rubbing alcohol (1 tablespoon of ink to 1 pint alcohol). When the wash dries, drybrush the bottom and top of the trunk with Polly S reefer white.

To assemble the trees, push the wafers over the top of the dowels, stacking them one on top of another, leaving a ¼" space between each wafer. Fasten each with a drop of white glue or Tacky glue. At planting time, put a drop of glue on the scenery and push the brad through it. Use a paint bottle to hold the trees upright until the glue dries.

DEAD WOOD, VINES, BRIAR PATCH, AND UNDERBRUSH

I cut one of the loofah sponges into small pieces and dyed them reddish

Toolbox of equipment

To make and plant trees:
- ✓ Soft-bristled brush
- ✓ Scissors
- ✓ Disposable latex gloves
- ✓ Serrated-edge knife
- ✓ White glue

brown, dark gray, and olive green. When ripped apart, the gray sponge makes convincing dead wood and bare branches for small trees or brush. Just glue a dead branch into a predrilled hole in the trunk. Larger pieces make good-looking driftwood for the waterfront. You can shred the brown sponge with scissors and use it as undergrowth or as the branch structure for small bushes. Spread the glue mixture and sprinkle on the sponge pieces.

After the glue dries, dab the tops of the loofah with a cotton swab dipped in white glue and sprinkle on green scenic foam or punched-paper leaves. Another use for brown sponge is to model seaweed. Just tear it apart and glue it to the rocks. Finish by painting it with gloss brown paint.

The reddish brown and olive green pieces make realistic briar patches. This is easy to model because all you have to do is pull and separate the sponge into a thin layer and glue it down. Loofah differs from most other natural scenery materials because it needs no further preservation, will not dry out, and is extremely tough.

GROUPING TREES FOR A NATURAL LOOK

Now for the magic that I spoke of at the beginning. You can enhance realism by planting the trees in groups. I like to mix tree types and colors, and plant three to five in a group. Just poke a hole in the scenery, squeeze on a drop of glue, and set the tree in place. Prop each tree straight with a heavy paint jar or bottle until the glue dries.

If you plan to model the Santa Fe or the Rio Grande Western, then you'll need a few cactus plants. Make these from a kit that contains cast resin pieces. Epoxy them together, spray them with green paint, and sprinkle on Noch yellow-green flocking while the paint is wet.

Don't forget to make a few trees to show that fall is on its way. This weed was covered with coarse red foam.

Use acrylic gloss medium to make the swiftly flowing water under the bridge. Paint several coats over a flat surface to make clear, hard water.

7 Modeling Water

Realistic ponds and streams on your model railroad are interesting scenic elements that are easy to make without using foul-smelling epoxies and resins.

In this chapter I'll show you how to use acrylic gloss medium to make convincing water surfaces. Gloss medium is a thick, white semiliquid that dries clear, hard, and glossy when brushed on the layout surface. Since it is water-soluble, cleanup is fast and easy.

MAKING A SMALL STREAM

With gloss medium you can add a stream anywhere on your model railroad. Of course, it'll look best if it's at, near, or heading toward the lowest spot on the layout. You can build the stream during any phase of scenery construction, or even after the scenery is complete.

To start, select a spot for the stream and remove some of the scenery base using a hobby knife. Be sure to dig away enough material to provide plenty of room for stones.

If you need special scenic contours, mix a small batch of Sculptamold and trowel it on. After 20 minutes or so, paint the new terrain with earth-color latex paint.

You'll need two or three grades of stones, from boulders down to fine sand, to line the stream bed. I like to use the larger pebbles sifted from a bag of contractor's sand because of their color. You should be able find suitable rocks at your hobby shop; large scale ballast can be used if you can find it in a color you like.

First, sprinkle the largest stones into the stream bed. Along the sides of the stream you may have to glue the stones in place to hold them. Next, sprinkle a finer gravel around the stones and on the stream bottom. Use a large soft brush to move the gravel here and there, especially under and around the larger stones. Finish by sprinkling the finest sand down the middle of the stream and along the banks—anywhere fast water would deposit it.

Using a spray bottle filled with wet water, mist the stones until they change color and the sand absorbs the water. Then, using a large eyedropper, soak the sand and stones with dilute white glue. Add glue until it starts to run off. Place paper towels around the edges to absorb any excess glue. Allow the glue to dry overnight, but remove the paper towels before they become stuck in place.

The next day check the stones to make sure they're all secure. If you find a few loose ones, refasten them with a drop of full-strength white glue.

COLORING THE STREAM BOTTOM

Make a dilute black wash by mixing six parts water with one part flat black latex paint. Flow this over and around the stones to darken the spaces between them. The idea is to color the scenery around and under the stones, not the stones themselves.

After the black wash dries, drybrush the tops of the stones using a wide, flat brush and your favorite earth-color paint. I use the earth color purchased for the rest of the scenery, thinned with equal parts of water,

then blended with enough white to make a light earth. Mix this as needed in a jar lid.

Here's the formula:
    1 part earth
    1 part water
    ½ part white

As you drybrush the tops of the stones and sand, watch how they seem to "pop" from the stream bed. Wait an hour or so for the paint to dry before adding the gloss medium water surface.

BRUSHING ON THE WET PART

Gloss medium looks like white mayonnaise and has about the same texture. As it dries it turns crystal clear. This can take from 30 minutes to several days, depending upon the thickness of the medium and whether your train room is dry or damp. (Acrylic gloss varnish will also work; both are available in art, craft, and hobby stores.)

To start making a small stream, remove some of the scenery base by cutting it away with a sharp knife. Make the stream bed deep enough that there's plenty of room for the stones. Brush Sculptamold over the raw Styrofoam to seal it.

Cover the white Sculptamold with earth-color paint to seal it and provide a base color for the stream.

Sprinkle stones into the stream bed and push them into place with a large brush. After gluing them in place, dry-brush the tops of the stones to make them stand out from the fast-flowing water.

Paint the bottom of this pond using only flat black and earth. Start by brushing the black in the center of the pond, then brush the earth-color paint out from the sides to meet it. Where the two colors meet, blend them with a brush dipped in water.

Working from the middle to the sides, brush the gloss medium into the stream bed. Make sure the medium flows over and under each stone. Even though the gloss medium is white when it's brushed on, it turns clear and glossy as it dries.

After applying several coats of gloss medium, color the fast-flowing water by streaking it with white. Over this apply another thick coat of gloss and allow it to dry for several days. The pipe gives the water someplace to come from.

You'll need to be careful as you brush the gloss medium into the stream bed. The first layer should be smooth and brushed around the stones, not over them. This is hard to do because it's the first coat and the stones are rough. If any medium gets on top of the rocks or somewhere else you don't want it, just wipe it away with a clean, wet brush, then scrub the area clean with water.

You'll need several coats of gloss medium to give the water the illusion of depth. If the stream has fast-flowing water, build up the height of the waves or rapids with each application. A light brushing of white paint behind the rocks can make great-looking froth and foam. Brush it between the layers of gloss medium. The medium will seal in the color and give it a glossy look.

As you apply successive coats of medium, sink in details so they'll look as if they're underwater. I added several tree branches, a couple of old tires, and several well-weathered logs. As you add more coats, you'll seal the details in place.

Gloss medium is very forgiving, so you can't make a mistake. If your waves are too high or the water looks too rough, grab a swatch of medium sandpaper and sand the surface smooth. Reapply more medium until the water looks right.

I discovered a good way to model lily pads by accident. I spilled about a teaspoon of Noch medium green paper flocking onto the wet gloss medium. I panicked and tried to blow it off the water. Of course, this just spread it downstream in a large, lopsided oval. When I stepped back to grab a hobby knife to scrape the flocking off the water, I noticed how good it looked as lily pads. I let the gloss medium dry overnight, then I vacuumed up any

These lily pads are the result of an accident. About a teaspoon of Noch medium green paper flocking spilled onto the wet gloss medium and there it stayed, stuck to the water.

In preparation for building a waterfall, glue large stones at the base of the falls and sprinkle smaller and smaller ones out into the river bottom. Over and around all the stones sprinkle fine sand, using the tea strainer. Then spray this with water and apply glue.

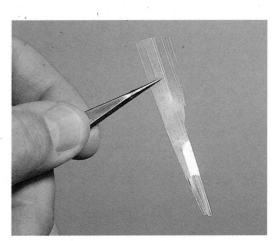

To model the falling water, use strips of clear plastic, scoring each strip so the strips can bend and conform to the contours of the rock without cracking.

flocking that did not stick—and marveled at my accidental lily pads.

MAKING A WATERFALL

A waterfall is simple to build, yet provides a strong focal point for your visitors. They'll all want to know your secret for success.

First, you need a mountainside that's high enough—at least 3 or 4 inches above the surrounding terrain. Higher is better, because height makes the falls more dramatic.

Test-fit the clear styrene strips so they will hang straight from the front edge of the top rock. Cup them to fit the curve on the front of the rock as well.

I made an area for the waterfall by building a rock face with one rock perpendicular to the others. This provides a shelf for the water to run over. I surrounded this rock with others, stacked to look as though water had worn them away. At the base of the falls I placed a handful of boulders (¼" to ½" round pebbles) and spread them with a large brush to look as though fast-moving water had pushed them into position. To hold the boulders in place I drizzled dilute white glue over them and left the glue to dry overnight, just as I did with the stream bed.

Using 5-minute epoxy, glue the strips to the front of the rock, holding them perpendicular to the ground until the epoxy sets. After about 10 minutes, brush another coat of epoxy over the rocks and the styrene to seal them together.

FALLING WATER

The falling water itself consists of strips of clear styrene covered with 5-minute epoxy. I used Evergreen .010 styrene, but any clear, stiff plastic will work.

Cut three strips of clear plastic, 1", 2", and 3" wide, each as long as the height of the falls. Randomly score each strip parallel with the edges. This allows the strips to bend and conform to the contours of the rock without breaking. The scored lines also help establish the look of rapidly running water.

Glue each strip to the overhanging lip of the rock with 5-minute epoxy. This part is tricky: You have to stand at the falls, prodding and holding the plastic in place, until the epoxy sets. The strips must hang straight down—nothing looks as phony as water defying gravity by falling sideways!

After the epoxy sets, mix another batch and brush it over the strips. Allow any excess to run off the falls and onto the rocks. Working in small batches, keep adding epoxy to the strips from top to bottom until the water has a thick, three-dimensional look. A strong side light will help you evaluate your progress. Smooth out any epoxy that falls on the rocks so the water won't form an unnatural-looking heap.

The finish coats on the waterfall are gloss acrylic medium. Brush it over

Brush the first coat of gloss medium over all the rocks and up into the area under the falls where water would splatter.

Streak the falls with white to simulate the turbulence of falling water.

Here, the whole streambed gets a second, heavy sealing coat of medium. It fills the areas between the stones and makes a surface for the next coloring step.

Toolbox of equipment

To make water:
- ✓ Large soft-bristled brush
- ✓ Turkey baster
- ✓ White glue
- ✓ Hobby knife
- ✓ Two-part, 5-minute epoxy

the falls and the rocks, pushing it into the cracks and crevices between the boulders. Apply the first layer so that it fills all the voids between the stones and seals the flat areas.

ADDING COLOR TO WATER

After the first coat dries, add some color. This will give the water depth and enhance the illusion that the waterfall is flowing swiftly. You'll need medium blue, medium green, black, and white acrylic colors, mixed in varying proportions with gloss medium.

Start by mixing equal parts of blue and green (about ½ teaspoon each) in a small dish. Put ½ teaspoon black on the other side of the dish. In yet another corner add about 2 tablespoons gloss medium, and pour some clean water into a separate dish for washing the brushes as you go along.

Stir together a little of the blue-green mixture and a small quantity of gloss medium and brush it at random around the stones on the river bottom. In the deeper areas, mix a little black with the blue and spread it between the stones to look like deep pools. If any of the color gets on top of the stones, dip the brush in the water and

After the gloss medium dries overnight, mix equal parts of acrylic blue and green with more gloss medium to simulate the color of cold, deep water. Brush this over and around the rocks. Wait until the medium dries clear before you evaluate the color. You can brush more paint around the stones if the color is not strong enough.

if the finished waterfall sits close to the backdrop, skew it toward the front of the layout so it can be seen.

wash it away. Add more black to the mixture to paint a shadow on the stream bottom under the bridge. When the blue has dried, streak pure white anywhere there's fast water: down the falls, between the rocks, and along the embankments.

The final step is to add several layers of gloss medium, allowing each to dry clear before adding the next. This will give the fast-moving water its shape. Use a very soft brush to spread the medium, taking care to leave waves and ripples. If your first waves don't look real or if they seem too high, just sand them down, brush away the dust, and try again.

As the water on your layout ages it's bound to get dirty. Fortunately, you can wash the surface of gloss medium with warm soapy water to revive it. If that doesn't do the trick, apply another layer of gloss medium to make the water like new again.

Make this little falls using the same techniques as the larger one, except that you'll use more 5-minute epoxy over the styrene on the falls itself. Brush on epoxy and allow it to set for 3 or 4 minutes before "teasing" it with the tip of a screwdriver.

Think of structures on a layout as props on a stage set. When they're carefully blended into the scenery, they give the scene realism.

8 Adding Details

Structures are scenery too! When you think of scenery you do need to think about how you'll include structures. Like props on a stage set, buildings are a vital part of your countryside. They make your layout look real. After the trains, structures are what your visitors notice most. Any time you spend blending structures with their surroundings will reward you tenfold, because it will make them an integral part of the scene.

Plastic structures, especially those that require some assembly, look okay when they're snapped together right from the box—but they'll look even better if they're lightly weathered to kill the plastic shine.

Most hi-rail modelers will want to use plastic structures as they come out of the box. These look okay when set in place on the layout, but they'll look even better if you add a bit of simple weathering. The weathering will kill the bright plastic look and blend the models with the dirt colors of your scenery. Weathering also allows you to choreograph how your visitors see the details on the structure. You can bring some forward and hide others. This trick is especially useful when you use inexpensive toy train structures that include oversized details.

GETTING OUT OF THE BOX

Remove the plastic structure or the kit pieces from the box and examine them for ill-fitting parts, misaligned pieces, large globs of flash (the plastic that squeezes between the mold halves), or other defects. Clean the pieces with a sanding block or flat file, or scrape the plastic with the edge of a hobby knife. If assembly is necessary, snap the parts together to check for tight fit and alignment. Set the structure on your layout, noting which side will face your visitors. This is the side you'll save for last after you've mastered the weathering techniques.

The first weathering technique employs chalk. It's the easiest medium to master because if you don't like

your results, you can simply wash away the chalk and try again.

I use soft pastel chalk. My favorite is the Grumbacher soft pastels landscape assortment, catalog no. 00/L. This set contains 30 different chalk sticks ranging from white through an assortment of earth colors to dark brown. Several shades of pastel blue and green are thrown in for good measure.

If you can't find this Grumbacher assortment in an art store a good alternative is the drawing chalks sold for kindergartners. I found an assortment in a craft store and selected black, white, brown, and several pastel earth shades. For fun I bought two shades of leaf green, a bright yellow, an orange, and a violet-red.

Both kinds of chalk are soft and easy to grind into the required fine powder. Work over a sheet of paper and rub a chalk stick on coarse

To make an assortment of several colors of weathering chalk, rub each stick on coarse sandpaper to make a pile of powder. Store each color in a 35mm film can or plastic bag.

Any kind of soft brush will work for weathering, including a no. 11 round-tip sable brush and an old shaving brush. Here a brown chalk is scrubbed onto the side of the model to simulate the effect of rain-splattered dirt.

sandpaper or a coarse file to make a pile of powder. Using the paper as a funnel, dump the powder into its own container. I use 35mm film cans or Zip-Loc plastic bags. Label each container so you can identify the color later.

You'll apply the chalk powder with brushes. I have several soft brushes that I use just for weathering, and I keep them with the powdered chalk. I use two different sizes, a no. 11 round-tip, sable brush for dusting small areas, and an old shaving brush for larger weathering jobs.

WEATHERING YOUR FIRST BUILDING

The Lionel passenger and freight station (no. 6-12734) is a good structure for your first attempt at pastel weathering. I started by brushing on earth-color chalk powder to simulate dirt that's kicked up onto the walls by rain. This is a band of dust around the base of the structure. I chose the station as the first weathering project because it has clapboard siding, which forms a natural divider and makes feathering the chalk powder much easier.

Use a watercolor mixing tray or a sheet of white typing paper as a palette to mix the chalk colors. Dump small piles of burnt umber and white chalk powder on to the palette, then pick up some of each color on the tip of your brush and mix them together until you have a light brown. Using the brush like a shovel, pick up some of the light brown powder and lightly brush it around the base of the structure from the bottom up.

Smooth the weathered areas of the structure into the unweathered areas by brushing upward with the shaving brush. You can also do this blending with your finger, but that's harder to control, and you run the risk

Weather the station roof using a mixture of white, green, tan, and burnt umber chalks. Mix all the colors together and apply them in bands, working from top to bottom.

Weather the platform using the same colors as on the roof, but take the process one step further—drybrush white over the chalk to bring out the texture of the boards.

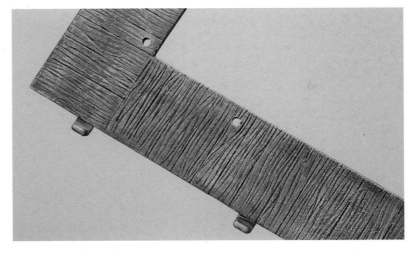

of leaving fingerprints on the model.

The station platform and the roof are next. You'll weather them using white, green, tan, and burnt umber mixed together. Mix them randomly in one big pile on the paper palette, or apply each color separately on the model. Remember to make your brush strokes parallel to the edges of the platform or roof. You can use the green chalk alone to model the effects of moss or mildew on old wood.

After I brush the power on a surface I sometimes set it by rubbing it lightly

A mixture of india ink and alcohol makes a wash for aging plastic structures. Just flow it on and let it run into the corners and around the framing.

If you paint the bricks a light color like yellow, you'll be able to apply a lot of weathering over it. The first step is to flow on the black wash. Tip the building upside down so the wash will flow under all the overhangs. When the wash dries, you can also flow a very dilute mix of Polly S white into the mortar lines to give the brick a more realistic appearance.

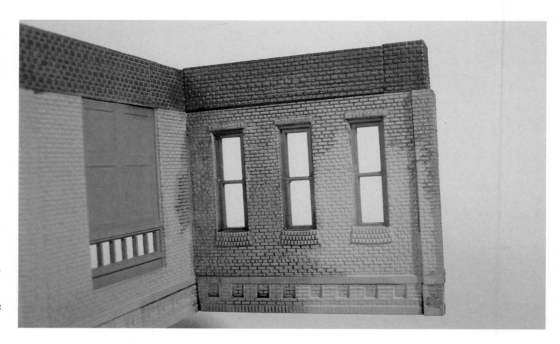

Drybrush all the doors and windows with white, then weather them lightly with chalk.

Paint the back of the window glazing before applying it to the structure.

Dark red is the hardest color to weather. Flow the black wash along the clapboards and let it run up under the edges of the boards.

Drybrush the upper edges of the clapboards. The white turns the red slightly pink and makes the boards look as if they've been faded by the sun.

with my finger. This removes excess the excess chalk and makes my fingers really dirty! Once you've got the hang of pastel weathering, try experimenting with this variation.

The final weathering is to use pure black chalk. This touch will set your structures apart. Load the black chalk powder on a brush and dab it up and under the eaves, roof overhang, windowsills, and any other place where you want to create a shadow. Painting in the shadows will give the structure and its details more depth and realism.

Don't be afraid to experiment. Weathering with pastels is easy to learn, but you've got to practice. Remember, if you don't like your results, just wash the chalk off the model and try again. When you're finally satisfied with the weathering, seal it in place permanently by spraying the structure with a flat varnish. There are many different brands and all work equally well. I like Dullcote, sold in hobby shops. You can also use any brand of matte fixative sold in art stores.

AGING PLASTIC STRUCTURES WITH INDIA INK

This method is more complicated than simply applying chalk, but it

Here's a finished boiler house, aged and weathered with all the techniques discussed. Notice how the roof was painted and weathered to look like old slate.

The roof is the first part of a structure folks see. Age a shingle roof like this with a heavy coating of brown chalk, then drybrush it with ivory.

Here's the finished structure buried in the foliage. Use a lot of trees to hide the seam between the building and the backdrop.

produces more realistic results. I selected a Design Preservation Models factory kit with brick walls and a plain roof.

Before assembly I removed all the flash from the pieces and primed them with a spray of flat gray automotive primer. The primer gives the castings a uniform color and matte surface, which is better for brush-painting.

After the pieces dry overnight, paint them with several Polly S acrylic colors. I used boxcar red on the brick walls, and colored the trim dark green. I mixed Polly S blue and green in equal proportions to make a slate color for the roof, and brushed it on using long vertical strokes.

After the paint dries, assemble the kit according to the instructions and set it in place on the layout to see how it looks. The back side of the building will be close to the backdrop and will face away from the front of the layout. This means you don't have to spend any time weathering this side because it will never be visible.

Bring the structure back to the workbench and tip it on its side. Here you'll apply a weathering wash made by adding 1 tablespoon india ink to ½ pint of 70 percent rubbing alcohol (**Warning:** Do not use this alcohol wash on a structure that has been sealed with Dullcote.) Fill the bottle with tap water to make one pint, then shake the mix well.

Test the wash on a piece of scrap plastic you've painted with Polly S and allowed to dry for several days. The alcohol wash should not soften or affect the paint in any way. If it does, add more water to the wash or let the paint dry longer.

Now apply the india ink mixture to one side of the building using a large, soft brush. Cover the whole side in one application, then tip the building

Blending a structure into the scenery is as easy as adding details around the foundation. Just about anything will work—piles of dirt, coal, dead leaves, or green grass. These details and more will hide the seam between the foundation and the layout.

bottom up so the ink runs up under window sills, ledges and overhangs. Let the wash dry. Repeat the treatment on the other two sides. (Remember, you're not doing the back.) Let each dry before starting the next. Note how the wash darkens and ages the colors.

The next step is drybrushing, which will slightly lighten the effects of the wash. Drybrushing is painting—very lightly—with a brush that's almost dry. It adds artificial highlights and emphasizes cast detail.

On this structure you'll be drybrushing with Polly S reefer white, but you can achieve equally effective results with ivory, tan, or gray. Some modelers drybrush with several different colors, each one a little lighter than the one before it.

You'll need a ½"-wide no. 12 square-tipped nylon brush, a palette (I use the plastic cover from a yogurt container), and a pad of paper towels.

Spread several drops of paint around the palette with the tip of the brush, then wipe the brush almost dry by scrubbing it on the pad of paper towels. To test for the correct amount of paint on the brush run the tip of the brush lightly down the fat part of the palm of your hand. Did it leave just a

little paint? Enough so that your skin texture is lightly accentuated? That is what you want. If the brush leaves a wide, wet mark on your palm, rub it again on the paper towel and try it again. (After several drybrushing sessions you'll know how much paint to rub off of the brush and you'll never have to paint your hand again.)

Now drybrush the factory roof. Start at the peak and work down (on a flat roof brush in the direction that water would flow). The rule when drybrushing is to work from top to bottom using parallel strokes. Use only light strokes,

The little piece of brick foundation was added to this structure to hide a dip in the scenery. It helps create the illusion that the structure's been sitting in the same spot for a long time. Also note the flowers, painted on the trellis with little dabs of red and yellow acrylic paint.

Wild Weeds make a variety of small weeds. Here's a hank of the Wild Weed material spread out on the workbench. Paint on a thick coat of Stiffy, a fabric-sizing chemical.

After the Stiffy dries, cut the Wild Weeds into strips. The sizing holds the pieces together.

Roll each piece into a cone and dip the top of the cone into the glue.

Then dip it into a mixture of coarse and fine foam.

leaving behind only a trace of color.

Work around the structure, dry-brushing each wall. Watch how the detail seems to pop out at you. If you make a mistake, take a damp pad of paper toweling and wipe it away. Dry-brushing is a great tool to show the detail and spruce up an otherwise dull building. After the drybrushing is finished, add more weathering with pastel chalks to suit the age of the structure.

BLENDING STRUCTURES INTO YOUR SCENERY

The easiest way to mount structures on your layout so they are removable

The finished bush waiting for planting. As this stage the glue is still wet, so you can't let go of it—it will try to flatten out.

Plant the bush by sticking it into full-strength white glue, then into a hole made with an awl. These weeds always need a little coaxing to stand up straight. Sometimes you have to place a paint bottle or other weight behind them to keep them erect.

The weed material can also be used in little sprigs. Grouping a lot of these weeds together gives a good effect.

day mark on the board where you want a walk, a grass plot, a sidewalk, shrubbery, and so forth.

Paint the areas marked for the walks and sidewalk with a coat of Polly S concrete. Next, brush full-strength white glue onto the areas where the grass and shrubs will be. Over the glue sprinkle green scenic foam for grass and brown foam against the house for dead leaves; add clumps of lichen for the shrubs.

After the glue is dry, tip the structure upside down over a wastebasket to remove excess texture material. Add extra detail, such as barrels on the loading dock, piles of lumber, a car in the driveway, people, and junk in the backyard.

Next place the structure on the layout and level it, if necessary. This is where the flat foam-core base comes in handy. You can shim it with cardboard until the structure is level. Then pick up the structure, apply white glue, and set the structure back on top of the shims. Add weights to the roof until the glue dries.

MAKING BUSHES, WEEDS, FLOWERS, AND WALLS

Bushes and shrubs are easy to model—you can use just about anything as long as it's green and fluffy.

is to mount each one on a piece of ¼" foam-core board. I do this at the workbench after the structure is painted and weathered. Where you place the structure will determine the size of the foam-core foundation. On some models the foam core will be the same size as the base of the structure; on others you'll want several extra inches on all sides of the building.

Start by measuring and cutting the foam-core slab and painting it with a coat of earth-color paint. When the paint dries, glue the structure to the board with white glue, Walther's Goo, or Pliobond. Place a weight on the structure and wait overnight. The next

Here's an easy way to make weeds from string. Wrap small sections of green string with masking tape and apply a drop of white glue above the tape. Cut each weed at the tape, trim it to shape with scissors, remove the tape, and plant it in the scenery.

This piece of a floor broom was used to make the cattails growing in a quiet area along side the track. Remove the bristles from the broom, dip the tips in glue, then dip them into brown foam.

Possible materials include lichen, Poly Fiber balls, and even green nylon pot-scrubber material that you have shredded, dipped in glue, and rolled in scenic foam. Use whatever material is at hand, as long as it's green and fluffy. Place the shrubs in clumps with every bush a different height for best results.

You can make hundreds of shrub-shaped bushes out of Timber Products Wild Weeds. This is a hairlike batting with a very fine texture. Cover the workbench with a piece of plastic wrap. Then remove a hank from the Wild Weeds bundle and smooth it flat on the plastic wrap. Brush on a light coat of dilute white glue or Stiffy, a fabric stiffener found in craft stores. When the glue dries it will hold the hank together.

Using scissors cut across the hank to make a piece that's 3 or 4 scale feet tall. These will be the branches that will hold the foliage. Tear away a small piece, roll it into a cone, and dip it in the dilute white glue. Drain the excess glue and plunge the tip into a box of coarse green scenic foam.

Lay each bush on a sheet of plastic wrap to dry. Plant the bushes by punching a hole in the scenery, adding a drop of white glue, and inserting the bush.

Weeds are just as easy to make. I've used all of the weed products sold commercially and I make my own weeds with string, yarn, and broom bristles. The string weeds are the easiest and quickest. Take a length of sisal

string (the coarse-textured string often used to bundle newspapers) that has been spray-painted a light green and mark off sections 3 or 4 scale feet long. Wrap a small piece of masking tape at each mark and add a drop of white glue above the tape.

The tape holds the string together and the glue seals it. When the glue dries, cut each section from the string just below the tape, remove the tape (the glue now hold it together) and trim it into a tapered weed shape. Plant them in clumps along with other types of weeds.

Flowers are the perfect addition if you want to add a spot of color to otherwise dull surroundings. You'll need an assortment of brightly colored scenic foam or several red and yellow felt-tip pens.

To make a field of flowers, glue down a fine sheet of Woodland Scenics FP178 Poly Fiber. Pull this material as fine as possible, spread a little dilute glue on the ground and push the Poly Fiber in place. After the glue dries, spray the surface of the Poly Fiber with hair spray and sprinkle on

the flowers. Several different colors together always look good. Add another coat of hair spray to seal the flowers in place.

Another way to make flowers where you can't use the spray is to "paint" them in place using red and yellow felt-tip pens. This works well on the side of a structure or on the tops of the bushes you've just built.

I wanted a few cattails along the sides of a pond I was building and didn't get around to making them until I discovered the perfect material for the tails—fiber broom bristles. They are the bristles on the wide brooms sold to sweep garages and factories. Look for the ones with brown fiber bristles. Remove a bundle of bristles and tape the bottom to hold them together. Dip the tops in full-strength white glue and then into brown scenic foam. After the glue dries, remove the tape and plant the cattails. I brushed a little dab of gloss medium around the base of the tails to hide the planting holes.

Stone walls are what I would call a little detail. "Little" because they're

People are a great addition to any layout. You can buy them painted or unpainted. To paint them, trim the plastic figures of flashing, prime them, then paint them using a small brush. Weather people on the station platform using the same techniques as you used on structures.

Simple details provide a small area of interest where your visitors stop, look, and comment.

quick to build and do not require any special materials. Just string out a pile of small stones—size is not important—along some boundary line, spray with wet water, and drizzle on the glue. After the glue dries add a sprig of lichen or other foliage here and there and you're done.

PAINTING PEOPLE

To add some life to your layout try painting people and animals. This is not as hard as it looks. The first step is to remove the flashing or parting lines by scraping with a hobby knife. Finish by sanding the seams smooth, then wash the figures in warm, soapy water to remove finger oils. After they're dry lay them on a sheet of newspaper in a well-ventilated area and spray with a can of gray automotive primer. Allow to air dry overnight, then glue the figures onto a block of wood to minimize handling.

Paint the hands, faces, and shoes first, followed by shirts, hair, and hats, and finish with large areas like overalls, suits, or dresses. I like to use water-soluble acrylics for all figure painting because the paint dries fast and is easy to control.

Toolbox of equipment

To add details:
- ✓ Lionel passenger and freight station no. 6-12734
- ✓ Sanding block (medium sandpaper)
- ✓ Hobby knife
- ✓ Large soft-bristled brush
- ✓ No. 11 round-tip sable brush
- ✓ Shaving brush
- ✓ No. 12 square-tipped nylon brush, ½" wide
- ✓ Lead weights
- ✓ White glue
- ✓ Scissors
- ✓ Masking tape

This layout-level shot shows the top of the backdrop. It is 15" high from the top of the layout and runs down the center to divide the layout into two viewing halves.

9 Behind the Scenes

The traditional place for the backdrop is behind your layout. You can mount it on the wall, on a free-standing frame, or on a combination of wall and framework.

But another place to put a backdrop is down the middle. You can practically double the visual impact of a walkaround layout by running a backdrop down its center. This divides the railroad into smaller, more interesting scenes, and their cumulative effect is to make the layout look larger.

BACKDROP MATERIALS

For a wall-mounted backdrop you can use Masonite, linoleum, or wallboard. For a backdrop that rests on the layout you'll need a lighter material. Such a backdrop must be lightweight and flexible, but stiff enough to stand by itself.

The product I choose most often nowadays is 3-mil (about 1/8"-thick) Komatex. This product, used for outdoor signs and displays, is available from plastic dealers. A flexible material similar to styrene, it comes in 4 x 8-foot sheets. It's easy to curve and cut, and accepts all types of paint without blistering or puckering. Komatex comes in white and several colors.

To determine the height of your backdrop, set a carpenter's square on the layout with the long leg pointing up in the air. Next, walk around and try to see over the upright leg. Fifteen inches from the layout surface seems to be about right—high enough that the average person viewing the layout can't see over it. If you settle on the 15" dimension, mark and cut two strips of backdrop material 15" wide x 8' long.

NO-TALENT BACKDROP PAINTING

Most modelers freeze up at the thought of painting a background. The association with art is strong, and most folks tend to wait for someone

Above: The backdrop is made from 3-mil-thick Komatex. Fasten the bottom to the top of the layout using a bead of Liquid Nails. Nail and glue blocks of wood on either side at 1-foot intervals.

Left: This is "no-talent backdrop painting." It's sky blue at the top blended into flat white at the bottom. In this photo the paint is still wet and needs more blending.

Right: To create the illusion of light, feathery clouds, mist the background with flat white spray paint. Hold the can far enough away from the background so that the paint "puffs" on. Here, the white was sprayed over the background hills as well.

else to come along and do the actual painting. But it doesn't take much art ability to make a decent-looking background. If I can do it, anybody can!

First, select a blue sky color that won't be so dark and deep that it overpowers the scene, yet not so light that it will look white and featureless in photos. I recommend you start with Sears no. 125 royal blue medium bright flat latex wall paint.

You can also have your sky color custom-mixed. Bring a sample or paint chip to the store and ask the clerk to mix several quarts (as many as you think you'll need plus an extra) of the color in flat interior latex. Semigloss will not work! While at the paint store buy a couple of quarts of flat white. You'll use this with the blue to paint a graduated sky.

If you feel adventurous and want to paint a few mountains and perhaps add some texture, pick up spray cans of flat white, flat light gray (auto body primer is okay), and several shades of flat green. You'll use them with simple cardboard cutout stencils to paint mountains.

Before you start painting, think about how the sky looks. If you go outside and look at the sky on a bright, cloudless day, you'll see that the sky directly overhead is deep blue, while the horizon is much lighter. I paint backgrounds with deep blue at the top, graduating to almost-white at the bottom. This strategy works for most parts of the country, except perhaps for a heavily polluted city scene, in which the color at the horizon would be more gray or yellow.

PAINTING YOUR BACKDROP

Wipe the background with a damp cloth to remove dust or dirt. Pour some blue paint into one paint roller tray and some white into another. Fill a shallow bowl about half full with water; it's the place to put your brush if the phone rings or nature calls, and you'll use the water to blend the colors on the background.

Use two 4" brushes. They're wide enough to apply the paint in long smooth strokes, and having two of them means you can blend the blue and white without having to clean the brush every two minutes. I've tried using rollers, and they're great for painting a very large background, but brushes are best for smaller layouts.

Start by applying the blue along the top of the background. Work from one end to the other, painting the blue down about one-third from the top. Apply the white as you did the blue, working from the bottom up.

Dip the white brush in the blue and paint a stripe of blue-white down the middle of the backdrop between the two colors. Blend this stripe up into the blue with the blue brush, using long horizontal strokes. Work from the middle down with the white brush, gradually changing the color from blue-white in the middle to white at the bottom.

An easy way to make complex-looking clouds is by using a stencil. This is just a piece of cardboard cut into cloud silhouettes. Hold it slightly away from the background and spray flat white paint lightly along the edge. Reverse the stencil and move it to make each cloud.

Make complex cloud effects very quickly using a variety of different-shaped stencils. Make these clouds in layers using both the positive and negative stencils.

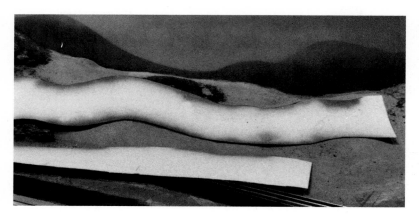

The easiest way to add mountains to the background is by using poster-board stencils. Use this simple stencil on either side to make hills with a variety of sizes and shapes.

Light gray and gray-green make the best colors for the most distant mountains, while the hill closest to the front of the layout should be almost all green.

This sounds complicated but it isn't. Just keep adding more white or blue until you have a smooth transition from one color to the other. A few lines or streaks where the colors meet are okay. To judge how it looks, just step back as far as you can and squint.

To smooth mistakes, dip a brush in the water, wipe it almost dry, and blend the colors with long, horizontal strokes. Some spots will require more paint, but add it cautiously. Too much paint will cause sags and runs.

Now let the paint dry. Evaluate your work the next day or after you've been away from it for a while.

ADDING CLOUDS

In a way, you added clouds (atmospheric haze) to the simple background just by blending white into the blue. You can take this one step further and add the illusion of light, feathery clouds by misting the background,

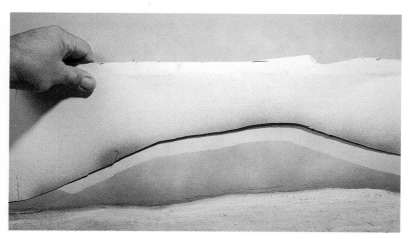

using a can of flat white spray paint. Hold the can far enough away from the background so that the paint "puffs" on. There will be a lot of overspray, so cover the layout with an old bedsheet or plastic drop cloth.

When you use spray paint indoors or out, wear a respirator! Spend the money to get one that removes paint particles, solvents, and other organic compounds from the air you breathe.

Spray the backdrop lightly, in long horizontal strokes. You're trying to add a streak of light haze up into the blue areas where it will be noticed. Practice your cloud-painting on an old piece of Masonite, Styrofoam, or other smooth surface until you get the hang of it.

MAKING STENCIL CLOUDS IS EASY

Another easy way to make great-looking clouds is with stencils. Draw a cloud-top outline along one edge of a sheet of cardboard or posterboard and cut it out with scissors. You can be as outrageous as you want, but keep the shapes smooth and rounded. Turn the cardboard on its side and make another cloud top, and continue until you have four different cloud stencils. (Thanks to John Lowrance and Miles Hale for the cloud stencil idea.)

Make a second set of stencils with different shapes. Now you'll have eight different stencils that you can use on either side, giving you 16 combinations. Along with your stencils you'll need a pair of latex gloves, several cans each of flat white and light gray spray paint, and your respirator.

Decide where the highest clouds will be. Some people like to paint the clouds at their eye level—and high clouds look great if your railroad is high, like a shelf-type layout. But if your layout is only 30" from the floor, you'll have to lower the clouds. I prefer to paint them about 12" above the layout's horizon line. High clouds made with stencils always look as if you were viewing them from above, looking down at them from an airplane.

Although there's only 2" between the rocks and the background hills, the white, hazy spray creates the illusion of great distance. Don't forget to cover track, structures, and your nose to protect them from the overspray.

Hold the stencil against the backdrop and lightly spray the flat white paint. Hold the can 12" to 14" from the backdrop. Spray lightly! These first clouds are the farthest from the viewer, and if you make them light and transparent they will look far away. Continue adding the distant clouds, using a different stencil for each one, until you get a sky you like.

Next, spray on the clouds that are one layer closer to the viewer. These can be whiter than the ones behind them, so spray on more paint. At the base of each cloud, spray a little gray, which will provide separation and contrast for the next bank of clouds.

I like to stagger the forward clouds between the peaks of those behind them. If you make a mistake (which is hard to do) just mist over it with white spray paint so it isn't as noticeable.

Keep adding layers. They don't have to be uniform, like row upon row of marching soldiers. They'll look better placed randomly. You don't have to use all of the stencil—you can use the most interesting areas over and over.

Try to paint all the clouds at one time, then go away and leave them for a while. The next day evaluate how they look. If some outlines look too hard, soften them a bit with a quick, horizontal spray of flat white.

DISTANT MOUNTAINS

The easiest way to add mountains to the background is with stencils. Cut four different mountain silhou-

ettes along the edges of a 30" x 40" piece of posterboard.

The colors for the mountains are important. The most distant should be a light gray-green color. The next closest should be a greener version of the distant mountains. And the closest (three layers of mountains seem to be enough) should almost all green. Choosing these colors premixed, in spray cans, can be difficult. I found many different shades of green in a craft store under the brand name Design Master.

If you have an airbrush and want to mix the colors yourself here are recipes for flat latex paint:

Most distant mountain range
    3 parts white
    1 part black
    1 part light green

White is the most important color in this formula. If the distant mountains seem too dark, add more white to the

Here's how to add three-dimensional hills to the backdrop. The foam putty mixture is dilute white glue mixed with enough scenic foam to make a soft putty. There's no exact formula: Just add glue or foam until the mixture holds together.

Press the putty lightly onto the backdrop to look like a distant tree-covered hill.

mixture. They should be only slightly darker than the sky behind them.

Mountains in the middle distance
    3 parts light green
    3 parts white
    1 part black
Closest mountain range
    3 parts light green
    1 part white
    1 part black

You can mix all three colors from the "most distant" color simply by adding more green to it. Be sure to mix enough "most distant" green to complete the background and spray on all the most distant mountains before adding more green to it. Always test new color combinations on scrap posterboard before applying them to your backdrop.

To begin, assemble the mountain stencils and spray cans or airbrush. Put on your respirator. You want the mountains to extend no more than halfway up the backdrop, so place the first stencil in position and spray on the "most distant" color. Feather the left and right edges so you can match the next stencil to the first.

Work your way completely around the backdrop, changing the stencils as you go, until you have painted all the most distant mountains. Some of these mountains will overlap the clouds, and this is okay, because it adds to the illusion of distance.

Using a spray can, gently mist a light dusting of flat white over the most distant mountains. This adds another cloud layer, which pushes the mountains further into the background.

FOAM PUTTY FOOTHILLS

The last step is to add three-dimensional hills to tie the backdrop to the foreground scenery. Mix one part white glue and three parts water with enough scenic foam to make a soft putty. There's no formula: Just add glue or foam until the mixture holds together.

Apply the foam putty with your fingers, pushing it against the backdrop so that it looks like the tops of tree-covered hills extending down to the foreground scenery. After the putty dries, glue in place small treetops made from Poly Fiber balls, followed by larger and larger trees.

Only 2 feet separates the foreground from the back, but the backdrop, with its distant mountains, greatly enhances the illusion that the layout goes on forever.

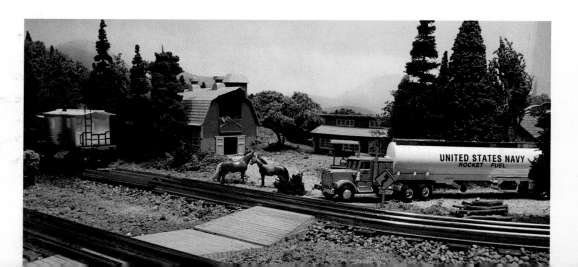

Appendix Suppliers and Manufacturers

American Art Clay Co.
4717 W. 16th St.
Indianapolis, IN 46222
Molding rubber, Sculptamold

AMSI Scale Model Supplies
115-B Bellam Boulevard
P. O. Box 3497
San Rafael, CA 94912
Scenery materials

Arttista
1616 S. Franklin St.
Philadelphia, PA 19148
Hand-painted action figures

Berkshire Valley Models
P. O. Box 150
Adams, MA 01220
Detail parts and buildings

Blue Ribbon Models
P. O. Box 333
Swampscott, MA 01907-3333
Rock molds

Boomtown Models
P. O. Box 181774
Dallas, TX 75218
Oil pumps, cactus

Bowser Mfg. Co.
21 Howard St.
P. O. Box 322
Montoursville, PA 17754-0322
Hand-painted figures, turntables

Buildings Unlimited
P. O. Box 239
Nazareth, PA 18064-0239
Buildings, railroad structures

Castle Studio
175 Fifth Ave., Suite 2674
New York, NY 10010
Street signs

Chooch Enterprises, Inc.
P. O. Box 217
Redmond, WA 98052
Detail parts

Classic Signs Ltd.
P. O. Box 1073
San Carlos, CA 94070-9998
Signs

Classic Toy Trains Magazine
21027 Crossroads Circle
P. O. Box 1612
Waukesha, WI 53187
The leading magazine for toy train collectors and operators

Design Preservation Models
P. O. Box 66

Linn Creek, MO 65052
Building kits

**Express Model
Landscaping Supplies**
P. O. Box 1594
Greensburg, PA 15601-6594
Scenery materials

Floquil-Polly S Color Corp.
Rt. 30 N.
Amsterdam, NY 12010
Paints

Grandt Line Products
1040-B Shary Ct.
Concord, CA 94518
Switchstands, detail parts

Highball Products Co.
P. O. Box 43633
Cincinnati, OH 45243
Track ballast

High Pines Ltd.
2015 Garst Circle
Boone, IA 50036
Pine trees

K & S Scenery Products
P. O. Box 117824
Carrollton, TX 75011-7824
Scenery materials

**Kalmbach Publishing
Co. / Greenberg Books Division**
21027 Crossroads Circle
P. O. Box 1612
Waukesha, WI, 53187
Model railroading books and magazines

K.B.'s Die-cast Direct
1009 Twilight Trail
Frankfort, KY 40601
Automobiles, trucks, tractors

Keil Line Models
6440 McCullom Lake Rd.
Wonder Lake, IL 60097
Signals, detail parts

K-Line Electric Trains
P. O. Box 2831
Chapel Hill, NC 27525
Locomotives, rolling stock, accessories

Kommerling USA Inc.
210 Summit Ave.
Montvale, NJ 07645
Background plastic

Kuras Design Group
112 Point Lobos Ave.
San Francisco, CA 94121
Rustall weathering system

Lexington Miniatures
P. O. Box 91
Lexington, IL 61753
Picnic benches, shelters, pallets

Lionel Trains, Inc.
50625 Richard W. Boulevard
Chesterfield, MI 48051-2493
Locomotives, rolling stock, accessories

Mainline Modules
P. O. Box 21861
Chattanooga, TN 37421-1861
Vinyl roadbed

Mike's Train House
9631-A Gerwig Lane
Columbia, MD 21046
Locomotives and rolling stock

Model Railroader Magazine
21017 Crossroads Circle
P. O. Box 1612
Waukesha, WI 53187
Leading model railroad magazine, serving all scales

Moondog Express
104 W. Ocean Ave.
Lompoc, CA 93436
Rubber ties, streets, track patterns

Oakridge Corp.
P. O. Box 247
Lemonte, IL 60439
Model railroad supplies

Plastruct
1020 S. Wallace Place
City of Industry, CA 91748
Oil tanks, plastic structural details

Selley Finishing Touches
21 Howard St.
Montoursville, PA 17754-0322
Detail accessories

Stevens International
P. O. Box 126
Magnolia, NJ 08049
Animals, people

Timber Products
2029 E. Howe Ave.
Tempe, AZ 85281
Scenery materials

Wm. K. Walthers Inc.
P. O. Box 18676
Milwaukee, WI 53218
Scenery materials

Woodland Scenics
P. O. Box 98
Linn Creek, MO 65052
Scenery materials, rock molds

Index